HERBERT BUTTERFIELD is Regius Professor of Modern
History at Cambridge University and Master of Peterhouse,
where he formerly was a student. He received an honorary
LL.D. at Aberdeen in 1952 and Hon. D.Litts. from Dublin
University (1954), Hong Kong (1961), Sheffield (1962), Hull
(1963), Belfast (1955), and Harvard and Columbia (1956).
From 1938-1952 he was Editor of the *Cambridge Historical
Journal* and from 1955-1958 he was President of the Historical Association. He is a Member of the Executive Board
of the International Association of Universities and was
Vice-Chancellor of the University of Cambridge from 1959 to
1961. His many books include *The Whig Interpretation of
History* (1931), *Napolean* (1939), *The Statecraft of Machiavelli* (1940), *The Origins of Modern Science* (1949), *Christianity and History* (1949), and *Man on his Past* (1955).

THE WHIG
INTERPRETATION
OF HISTORY

H. BUTTERFIELD, M.A.

The Norton Library
W · W · NORTON & COMPANY · INC ·
NEW YORK

FOR

PAUL VELLACOTT

All Rights Reserved

FIRST PUBLISHED IN THE NORTON LIBRARY 1965

ISBN 0   393   00318 3

PRINTED IN THE UNITED STATES OF AMERICA

7 8 9 0

PREFACE

THE following study deals with 'the whig interpretation of history' in what I conceive to be the accepted meaning of the phrase. At least it covers all that is ordinarily understood by the words, though possibly it gives them also an extended sense. What is discussed is the tendency in many historians to write on the side of Protestants and Whigs, to praise revolutions provided they have been successful, to emphasise certain principles of progress in the past and to produce a story which is the ratification if not the glorification of the present. This whig version of the course of history is associated with certain methods of historical organisation and inference – certain fallacies to which all history is liable, unless it be historical research. The examination of these raises problems concerning the relations between historical research and what is known as general history; concerning the nature of a historical transition and of what might be called the historical process; and also concerning the limits of history as a study, and particularly the attempt of the whig writers to gain from it a finality that it cannot give.

The subject is treated not as a problem in the philosophy of history, but rather as an aspect of the psychology of historians. Use has been made of words like conjuncture and contingency to describe what appear as such to the observer and to the historian. The present study does not concern itself with the philosophical description or analysis of these. And its theses would be unaffected by anything the philosopher could state to explain them or to explain them away.

H. B.

September, 1931

CONTENTS

I. INTRODUCTION

It has been said that the historian is the avenger, and that standing as a judge between the parties and rivalries and causes of bygone generations he can lift up the fallen and beat down the proud, and by his exposures and his verdicts, his satire and his moral indignation, can punish unrighteousness, avenge the injured or reward the innocent. One may be forgiven for not being too happy about any division of mankind into good and evil, progressive and reactionary, black and white; and it is not clear that moral indignation is not a dispersion of one's energies to the great confusion of one's judgment. There can be no complaint against the historian who personally and privately has his preferences and antipathies, and who as a human being merely has a fancy to take part in the game that he is describing; it is pleasant to see him give way to his prejudices and take them emotionally, so that they splash into colour as he writes; provided that when he steps in this way into the arena he recognises that he is stepping into a world of partial judgments and purely personal appreciations and does not imagine that he is speaking *ex cathedra*. But if the historian can rear himself up like a god and judge, or stand as the official avenger of the crimes of the past, then one can require that he shall be still more godlike and regard himself rather as the reconciler than as the avenger; taking it that his aim is to achieve the understanding of the men and parties and causes of the past, and that in this understanding, if it can be complete, all things will ultimately be reconciled. It seems to be assumed that in history we can have something more than the private points of view of particular historians; that there are 'verdicts of history' and that history itself, considered impersonally, has something to say to men. It seems to be accepted that each historian does something more than make a confession of his private mind and his whimsicalities, and that all of them are trying to elicit a truth, and perhaps combining through their various imperfections to express a truth, which, if we could perfectly attain it, would be the voice of

History itself. But if history is in this way something like the memory of mankind and represents the spirit of man brooding over man's past, we must imagine it as working not to accentuate antagonisms or to ratify old party-cries but to find the unities that underlie the differences and to see all lives as part of the one web of life. The historian trying to feel his way towards this may be striving to be like a god but perhaps he is less foolish than the one who poses as god the avenger. Studying the quarrels of an ancient day he can at least seek to understand both parties to the struggle and he must want to understand them better than they understood themselves; watching them entangled in the net of time and circumstance he can take pity on them — these men who perhaps had no pity for one another; and, though he can never be perfect, it is difficult to see why he should aspire to anything less than taking these men and their quarrels into a world where everything is understood and all sins are forgiven.

It is astonishing to what an extent the historian has been Protestant, progressive, and whig, and the very model of the 19th

century gentleman.   Long after he became
a determinist he retained his godly rôle as
the dispenser of moral judgments, and like
the disciples of Calvin he gave up none
of his right to moral indignation. Even when
he himself has been unsympathetic to the
movements of his own generation, as in the
case of Hallam, who bitterly opposed the
Great Reform Bill and trembled to think of the
revolutionary ways into which the country was
moving, something in his constitution still
makes him lean to what might be called the
whig interpretation of history, and he refuses
historical understanding to men whose attitude
in the face of change and innovation was
analogous to his own.   It might be argued that
our general version of the historical story still
bears the impress that was given to it by the
great patriarchs of history-writing, so many of
whom seem to have been whigs and gentlemen
when they have not been Americans: and
perhaps it is from these that our textbook
historians have inherited the top hat and the
pontifical manner, and the grace with which
they hand out a consolation prize to the man
who, 'though a reactionary, was irreproachable

in his private life.' But whether we take the contest of Luther against the popes, or that of Philip II and Elizabeth, or that of the Huguenots with Catherine de' Medici; whether we take Charles I versus his parliaments or the younger Pitt versus Charles James Fox, it appears that the historian tends in the first place to adopt the whig or Protestant view of the subject, and very quickly busies himself with dividing the world into the friends and enemies of progress. It is true that this tendency is corrected to some extent by the more concentrated labours of historical specialists, but it is remarkable that in all the examples given above, as well as in many others, the result of detailed historical research has been to correct very materially what had been an accepted Protestant or whig interpretation. Further, this whig tendency is so deep-rooted that even when piece-meal research has corrected the story in detail, we are slow in re-valuing the whole and reorganising the broad outlines of the theme in the light of these discoveries; and what M. Romier has deplored in the historians of the Huguenots might fairly be imputed to those in other fields

of history; that is, the tendency to patch the
new research into the old story even when the
research in detail has altered the bearings of
the whole subject.   We cling to a certain
organisation of historical knowledge which
amounts to a whig interpretation of history,
and all our deference to research brings us
only to admit that this needs qualifications in
detail. But exceptions in detail do not prevent
us from mapping out the large story on the
same pattern all the time; these exceptions are
lost indeed in that combined process of
organisation and abridgment by which we
reach our general survey of general history;
and so it is over large periods and in reference
to the great transitions in European history
that the whig view holds hardest and holds
longest; it is here that we see the results of a
serious discrepancy between the historical
specialist and what might be called the general
historian.

The truth is that there is a tendency for all
history to veer over into whig history, and this
is not sufficiently explained if we merely
ascribe it to the prevalence and persistence of a
traditional interpretation.   There is a magnet

for ever pulling at our minds, unless we have
found the way to counteract it; and it may be
said that if we are merely honest, if we are not
also carefully self-critical, we tend easily to be
deflected by a first fundamental fallacy. And
though this may even apply in a subtle way to
the detailed work of the historical specialist,
it comes into action with increasing effect the
moment any given subject has left the hands
of the student in research; for the more we are
discussing and not merely enquiring, the more
we are making inferences instead of researches, then the more whig our history
becomes if we have not severely repressed our
original error; indeed all history must tend to
become more whig in proportion as it becomes
more abridged.   Further, it cannot be said
that all faults of bias may be balanced by work
that is deliberately written with the opposite
bias; for we do not gain true history by merely
adding the speech of the prosecution to the
speech for the defence; and though there have
been Tory – as there have been many Catholic
– partisan histories, it is still true that there is
no corresponding tendency for the subject
itself to lean in this direction; the dice cannot

be secretly loaded by virtue of the same kind of original unconscious fallacy. For this reason it has been easy to believe that Clio herself is on the side of the whigs.

II. THE UNDERLYING ASSUMPTION

THE primary assumption of all attempts to understand the men of the past must be the belief that we can in some degree enter into minds that are unlike our own. If this belief were unfounded it would seem that men must be for ever locked away from one another, and all generations must be regarded as a world and a law unto themselves. If we were unable to enter in any way into the mind of a present-day Roman Catholic priest, for example, and similarly into the mind of an atheistical orator in Hyde Park, it is difficult to see how we could know anything of the still stranger men of the sixteenth century, or pretend to understand the process of history-making which has moulded us into the world of to-day. In reality the historian postulates that the world is in some sense always the same world and that even the men most dissimilar are never absolutely unlike. And though a sentence from Aquinas may fall so strangely upon modern ears that it becomes plausible to dismiss

the man as a fool or a mind utterly and absolutely alien, I take it that to dismiss a man in
this way is a method of blocking up the mind
against him, and against something important
in both human nature and its history; it is
really the refusal to a historical personage of
the effort of historical understanding. Precisely because of his unlikeness to ourselves
Aquinas is the more enticing subject for the
historical imagination; for the chief aim of the
historian is the elucidation of the unlikenesses
between past and present and his chief function is to act in this way as the mediator between other generations and our own. It is
not for him to stress and magnify the similarities between one age and another, and he is
riding after a whole flock of misapprehensions
if he goes to hunt for the present in the past.
Rather it is his work to destroy those very
analogies which we imagined to exist. When
he shows us that Magna Carta is a feudal docu-
ment in a feudal setting, with implications
different from those we had taken for granted,
he is disillusioning us concerning something
in the past which we had assumed to be too
like something in the present.   That whole

process of specialised research which has in so many fields revised the previously accepted whig interpretation of history, has set our bearings afresh in one period after another, by referring matters in this way to their context, and so discovering their unlikeness to the world of the present-day.

It is part and parcel of the whig interpretation of history that it studies the past with reference to the present; and though there may be a sense in which this is unobjectionable if its implications are carefully considered, and there may be a sense in which it is inescapable, it has often been an obstruction to historical understanding because it has been taken to mean the study of the past with direct and perpetual reference to the present. Through this system of immediate reference to the present-day, historical personages can easily and irresistibly be classed into the men who furthered progress and the men who tried to hinder it ; so that a handy rule of thumb exists by which the historian can select and reject, and can make his points of emphasis. On this system the historian is bound to construe his function as demanding him to be vigilant for likenesses between past and present, instead of being vigilant for unlikenesses; so that he will find it easy to say that he has seen the present in the past, he will imagine that he has discovered a 'root' or an 'anticipation' of the 20th century, when in reality he is in a world of different connotations altogether, and he has merely tumbled upon what could be shown to be a misleading analogy. ·Working upon the same system the whig historian can draw lines through certain events, some such line as that which leads through Martin Luther and a long succession of whigs to modern liberty; and if he is not careful he begins to forget that this line is merely a mental trick of his; he comes to imagine that it represents something like a line of causation. The total result of this method is to impose a certain form upon the whole historical story, and to produce a scheme of general history which is bound to converge beautifully upon the present – all demonstrating throughout the ages the workings of an obvious principle of progress, of which the Protestants and whigs have been the perennial allies while Catholics and tories have perpetually formed obstruction.

A caricature of this result is to be seen in a popular view that is still not quite eradicated: the view that the Middle Ages represented a period of darkness when man was kept tongue-tied by authority – a period against which the Renaissance was the reaction and the Reformation the great rebellion. It is illustrated to perfection in the argument of a man denouncing Roman Catholicism at a street corner, who said: 'When the Pope ruled England them was called the Dark Ages.'

The whig historian stands on the summit of the 20th century, and organises his scheme of history from the point of view of his own day; and he is a subtle man to overturn from his mountain-top where he can fortify himself with plausible argument. He can say that events take on their due proportions when observed through the lapse of time. He can say that events must be judged by their ultimate issues, which, since we can trace them no farther, we must at least follow down to the present. He can say that it is only in relation to the 20th century that one happening or another in the past has relevance or significance for us. He can use all the arguments that are so handy to men when discussion is dragged into the market place and philosophy is dethroned by common sense; so that it is no simple matter to demonstrate how the whig historian, from his mountain-top, sees the course of history only inverted and aslant. The fallacy lies in the fact that if the historian working on the 16th century keeps the 20th century in his mind, he makes direct reference across all the intervening period between Luther or the Popes and the world of our own day. And this immediate juxtaposition of past and present, though it makes everything easy and makes some inferences perilously obvious, is bound to lead to an over-simplification of the relations between events and a complete misapprehension of the relations between past and present.

This attitude to history is not by any means the one which the historical specialist adopts at the precise moment when he is engaged upon his particular research; and indeed as we come closer to the past we find it impossible to follow these principles consistently even though we may have accepted them verbally. In spite of ourselves and in spite of our

theories we forget that we had set out to study
the past for the sake of the present, we cannot
save ourselves from tumbling headlong into
it and being immersed in it for its own sake;
and very soon we may be concentrated upon
the most useless things in the world – Marie
Antoinette's ear-rings or the adventures of the
Jacobites. But the attitude is one which we
tend to adopt when we are visualising the
general course of history or commenting on it,
and it is one into which the specialist himself
often slides when he comes to the point of
relating his special piece of work to the larger
historical story. In other words it represents
a fallacy and an unexamined habit of mind
into which we fall when we treat of history on
the broad scale. It is something which inter-
venes between the work of the historical
specialist and that work, partly of organisation
and partly of abridgment, which the general
historian carries out; it inserts itself at the
change of focus that we make when we pass
from the microscopic view of a particular
period to our bird's-eye view of the whole;
and when it comes it brings with it that whig
interpretation of history which is so different

from the story that the research student has to tell.

There is an alternative line of assumption upon which the historian can base himself when he comes to his study of the past; and it is the one upon which he does seem more or less consciously to act and to direct his mind when he is engaged upon a piece of research. On this view he comes to his labours conscious of the fact that he is trying to understand the past for the sake of the past, and though it is true that he can never entirely abstract himself from his own age, it is none the less certain that this consciousness of his purpose is a very different one from that of the whig historian, who tells himself that he is studying the past for the sake of the present. Real historical understanding is not achieved by the subordination of the past to the present, but rather by our making the past our present and attempting to see life with the eyes of another century than our own. It is not reached by assuming that our own age is the absolute to which Luther and Calvin and their generation are only relative; it is only reached by fully accepting the fact that their generation was as valid as our generation, their issues as momentous as our issues and their day as full and as vital to them as our day is to us. The twentieth century which has its own hairs to split may have little patience with Arius and Athanasius who burdened the world with a quarrel about a diphthong, but the historian has not achieved historical understanding, has not reached that kind of understanding in which the mind can find rest, until he has seen that that diphthong was bound to be the most urgent matter in the universe to those people. It is when the emphasis is laid in this way upon the historian's attempt to understand the past, that it becomes clear how much he is concerned to elucidate the unlikenesses between past and present. Instead of being moved to indignation by something in the past which at first seems alien and perhaps even wicked to our own day, instead of leaving it in the outer darkness, he makes the effort to bring this thing into the context where it is natural, and he elucidates the matter by showing its relation to other things which we do understand. Whereas the man who keeps his eye on the present tends to ask some such

question as, How did religious liberty arise ?
while the whig historian by a subtle organisation of his sympathies tends to read it as the
question, To whom must we be grateful for
our religious liberty ? the historian who is
engaged upon studying the 16th century at
close hand is more likely to find himself asking why men in those days were so given to
persecution. This is in a special sense the
historian's question for it is a question about
the past rather than about the present, and in
answering it the historian is on his own
ground and is making the kind of contribution
which he is most fitted to make. It is in this
sense that he is always forgiving sins by the
mere fact that he is finding out why they
happened. The things which are most alien
to ourselves are the very object of his exposition. And until he has shown why men
persecuted in the 16th century one may doubt
whether he is competent to discuss the further
question of how religious liberty has come
down to the 20th.

But after this attempt to understand the
past the historian seeks to study change taking
place in the past, to work out the manner in

which transitions are made, and to examine the way in which things happen in this world. If we could put all the historians together and look at their total co-operative achievement they are studying all that process of mutation which has turned the past into our present. And from the work of any historian who has concentrated his researches upon any change or transition, there emerges a truth of history which seems to combine with a truth of philosophy. It is nothing less than the whole of the past, with its complexity of movement, its entanglement of issues, and its intricate interactions, which produced the whole of the complex present; and this, which is itself an assumption and not a conclusion of historical study, is the only safe piece of causation that a historian can put his hand upon, the only thing which he can positively assert about the relationship between past and present. When the need arises to sort and disentangle from the present one fact or feature that is required to be traced back into history, the historian is faced with more unravelling than a mind can do, and finds the network of inter-actions so intricate, that it is impossible to point to any one thing in the sixteenth century as the cause of any one thing in the twentieth. It is as much as the historian can do to trace with some probability the sequence of events from one generation to another, without seeking to draw the incalculably complex diagram of causes and effects for ever interlacing down to the third and fourth generations. Any action which any man has ever taken is part of that whole set of circumstances which at a given moment conditions the whole mass of things that are to happen next. To understand that action is to recover the thousand threads that connect it with other things, to establish it in a system of relations; in other words to place it in its historical context. But it is not easy to work out its consequences, for they are merged in the results of everything else that was conspiring to produce change at that moment. We do not know where Luther would have been if his movement had not chimed with the ambitions of princes. We do not know what would have happened to the princes if Luther had not come to their aid.

The volume and complexity of historical

research are at the same time the result and
the demonstration of the fact that the more we
examine the way in which things happen, the
more we are driven from the simple to the
complex. It is only by undertaking an actual
piece of research and looking at some point in
history through the microscope that we can
really visualise the complicated movements
that lie behind any historical change. It is
only by this method that we can discover the
tricks that time plays with the purposes of
men, as it turns those purposes to ends not
realised; or learn the complex processes by
which the world comes through a transition
that seems a natural and easy step in progress
to us when we look back upon it. It is only
by this method that we can come to see the
curious mediations that circumstances must
provide before men can grow out of a complex
or open their minds to a new thing. Perhaps
the greatest of all the lessons of history is this
demonstration of the complexity of human
change and the unpredictable character of the
ultimate consequences of any given act or
decision of men; and on the face of it this is
a lesson that can only be learned in detail. It

is a lesson that is bound to be lost in abridgment, and that is why abridgments of history are sometimes calculated to propagate the very reverse of the truth of history. The historian seeks to explain how the past came to be turned into the present but there is a very real sense in which the only explanation he can give is to unfold the whole story and reveal the complexity by telling it in detail. In reality the process of mutation which produced the present is as long and complicated as all the most lengthy and complicated works of historical research placed end to end, and knit together and regarded as one whole.

The fallacy of the whig historian lies in the way in which he takes his short cut through this complexity. The difficulty of the general historian is that he has to abridge and that he must do it without altering the meaning and the peculiar message of history. The danger in any survey of the past is lest we argue in a circle and impute lessons to history which history has never taught and historical research has never discovered – lessons which are really inferences from the particular organisation that we have given to our knowledge.

We may believe in some doctrine of evolution
or some idea of progress and we may use this
in our interpretation of the history of centuries;
but what our history contributes is not evolution but rather the realisation of how crooked
and perverse the ways of progress are, with
what wilfulness and waste it twists and turns,
and takes anything but the straight track to
its goal, and how often it seems to go astray,
and to be deflected by any conjuncture, to
return to us – if it does return – by a back-
door. We may believe in some providence
that guides the destiny of men and we may if
we like read this into our history; but what
our history brings to us is not proof of providence but rather the realisation of how myster-
ious are its ways, how strange its caprices –
the knowledge that this providence uses any
means to get to its end and works often at
cross-purposes with itself and is curiously
wayward. Our assumptions do not matter if
we are conscious that they are assumptions,
but the most fallacious thing in the world is to
organise our historical knowledge upon an
assumption without realising what we are
doing, and then to make inferences from that

organisation and claim that these are the voice of history. It is at this point that we tend to fall into what I have nicknamed the whig fallacy.

The whig method of approach is closely connected with the question of the abridgment of history; for both the method and the kind of history that results from it would be impossible if all the facts were told in all their fullness. The theory that is behind the whig interpretation – the theory that we study the past for the sake of the present – is one that is really introduced for the purpose of facilitating the abridgment of history; and its effect is to provide us with a handy rule of thumb by which we can easily discover what was important in the past, for the simple reason that, by definition, we mean what is important 'from our point of view.' No one could mistake the aptness of this theory for a school of writers who might show the least inclination to undervalue one side of the historical story; and indeed there would be no point in holding it if it were not for the fact that it serves to simplify the study of history by providing an excuse for leaving things out. The theory is important because it provides us in the long run with a path through the complexity of history; it really gives us a short cut through that maze of interactions by which the past was turned into our present; it helps us to circumvent the real problem of historical study. If we can exclude certain things on the ground that they have no direct bearing on the present, we have removed the most troublesome elements in the complexity and the crooked is made straight. There is no doubt that the application of this principle must produce in history a bias in favour of the whigs and must fall unfavourably on Catholics and tories. Whig history in other words is not a genuine abridgment, for it is really based upon what is an implicit principle of selection. The adoption of this principle and this method commits us to a certain organisation of the whole historical story. A very different case arises when the historian, examining the 16th century, sets out to discover the things which were important to that age itself or were influential at that time. And if we could imagine a general survey of the centuries which should be an abridgment of all the works of historical research, and if we were then to compare this with a survey of the whole period which was compiled on the whig principle, that is to say, 'from the point of view of the present,' we should not only find that the complications had been greatly over-simplified in the whig version, but we should find the story recast and the most important valuations amended; in other words we should find an abridged history which tells a different story altogether. According to the consistency with which we have applied the principle of direct reference to the present, we are driven to that version of history which is called the whig interpretation.

Seeing Protestant fighting Catholic in the 16th century we remember our own feelings concerning liberty in the 20th, and we keep before our eyes the relative positions of Catholic and Protestant to-day. There is open to us a whole range of concealed inference based upon this mental juxtaposition of the 16th century with the present; and, even before we have examined the subject closely, our story will have assumed its general shape; Protestants will be seen to have been fighting for the future, while it will be obvious that the

Catholics were fighting for the past. Given this original bias we can follow a technical procedure that is bound to confirm and imprison us in it; for when we come, say, to examine Martin Luther more closely, we have a magnet that can draw out of history the very things that we go to look for, and by a hundred quotations torn from their context and robbed of their relevance to a particular historical conjuncture we can prove that there is an analogy between the ideas of Luther and the world of the present day, we can see in Luther a foreshadowing of the present. History is subtle lore and it may lock us in the longest argument in a circle that one can imagine. It matters very much how we start upon our labours – whether for example we take the Protestants of the 16th century as men who were fighting to bring about our modern world, while the Catholics were struggling to keep the mediæval, or whether we take the whole present as the child of the whole past and see rather the modern world emerging from the clash of both Catholic and Protestant. If we use the present as our perpetual touchstone, we can easily divide the men of the 16th

century into progressive and reactionary; but
we are likely to beg fewer questions, and we
are better able to discover the way in which
the past was turned into our present, if we
adopt the outlook of the 16th century upon
itself, or if we view the process of events as it
appears to us when we look at the movements
of our own generation; and in this case we shall
tend to see not so much progressive fighting
reactionary but rather two parties differing on
the question of what the next step in progress
is to be.   Instead of seeing the modern world
emerge as the victory of the children of light
over the children of darkness in any generation, it is at least better to see it emerge as the
result of a clash of wills, a result which often
neither party wanted or even dreamed of, a
result which indeed in some cases both parties
would equally have hated, but a result for the
achievement of which the existence of both and
the clash of both were necessary.

The whig historian has the easier path
before him and his is the quicker way to heavy
and masterly historical judgments; for he is in
possession of a principle of exclusion which
enables him to leave out the most troublesome

element in the complexity. By seizing upon those personages and parties in the past whose ideas seem the more analogous to our own, and by setting all these out in contrast with the rest of the stuff of history, he has his organisation and abridgment of history ready-made and has a clean path through the complexity. This organisation of his history will answer all questions more clearly than historical research is ever able to do. It will enable him, even before he has studied anything very deeply, to arrive at what seem to be self-evident judgments concerning historical issues. It will enable him to decide irrevocably and in advance, before historical research has said anything and in the face of anything it might say, that Fox, whatever his sins, was fighting to save liberty from Pitt, while Pitt, whatever his virtues, cannot be regarded as fighting to save liberty from Fox. But it is the thesis of this essay that when we organise our general history by reference to the present we are producing what is really a gigantic optical illusion; and that a great number of the matters in which history is often made to speak with most certain voice, are not inferences made from the past but are inferences made from a particular series of abstractions from the past – abstractions which by the very principle of their origin beg the very questions that the historian is pretending to answer. It is the thesis of this essay that the Protestant and whig interpretation of history is the result of something much more subtle than actual Protestant or party bias; the significant case arises when the very men who opposed votes for women until the vote could be withheld no longer, are unable to see in the opponents of the Great Reform Bill anything but the corrupt defenders of profitable abuses; and it is this kind of limitation to the effort of historical understanding which requires to be explained. The whig interpretation of history is not merely the property of whigs and it is much more subtle than mental bias; it lies in a trick of organisation, an unexamined habit of mind that any historian may fall into. It might be called the historian's 'pathetic fallacy.' It is the result of the practice of abstracting things from their historical context and judging them apart from their context – estimating them and organising the historical story by a system of direct reference to the present.

It may be argued that this whig principle which is under discussion is seldom applied by any historian with prolonged consistency; and one might go further and say that it could not conceivably be applied with perfect completeness. Its logical conclusion, if it had any, would be the study of the present without reference to the past; a consummation which is indeed approached, if we can judge by some of the best specimens of the fallacy — the case of some popular views in regard to the Dark Ages, for example. This whig principle accounts for many of the common misconceptions concerning the past, but its application is by no means restricted to the region of popular error; witness the fact that it can be put forward as a definite theory by historians. It represents a kind of error into which it is very difficult for us not to fall; but, more than this, it is the very sum and definition of all errors of historical inference. The study of the past with one eye, so to speak, upon the present is the source of all sins and sophistries in history, starting with the simplest of them,

the anachronism. It is the fallacy into which
we slip when we are giving the judgments that
seem the most assuredly self-evident. And it
is the essence of what we mean by the word
'unhistorical.' It describes the attitude by
which the men of the Renaissance seem to
have approached the Middle Ages. It describes the attitude of the 18th century to many
a period of the past. It accounts for a good
deal of the plausibility of that special form of
the whig interpretation which expounded the
history of England in the light of the theory
of primitive Germanic freedom. It explains a
hundred whig and Protestant versions of
history that have been revised by the work of
specialists. And though it might be said that
in any event all errors are corrected by more
detailed study, it must be remembered that
the thesis itself is one that has the effect of
stopping enquiry; as against the view that we
study the past for the sake of the past, it is
itself an argument for the limitation of our
aims and our researches; it is the theory that
history is very useful provided we take it in
moderation; and it can be turned into an
apology for anything that does not tally with

historical research. A more intensive study can only be pursued, as has been seen, in proportion as we abandon this thesis. And even so, even in the last resort, though a further enquiry has corrected so many of the more glaring errors that result from this fallacy, there is a sense in which, if we hold to the whig thesis, historical research can never catch up, for it can never break into the circle in which we are arguing. The specialist himself is cheated and he cries out to us to no purpose, if we re-cast his work from what we call the point of view of the present — still selecting what conforms to our principle, still patching the new research into the old story.

III. THE HISTORICAL PROCESS

THE whig method of approach is bound to lead
to an over-dramatisation of the historical
story; it tends to make the historian miscon-
ceive both parties to any struggle that takes
place in any given generation. The party that
is more analogous to the present is taken to
be more similar, more modern than close
examination would justify, for the simple
reason that the historian is concentrating
upon likenesses and is abstracting them from
their context and is making them his points of
emphasis. The result is that to many of us
the sixteenth century Protestants or the whigs
of 1800 seem much more modern than they
really were, and even when we have corrected
this impression by closer study we find it
difficult to keep in mind the differences
between their world and ours. At worst some
people seem willing to believe that Luther was
a modern Protestant fighting for a broader
and more liberal theology against the religious
fanaticism of Rome; although heaven itself

might bear witness that it was anything but the religious fanaticism of the Renaissance popes that drove Luther to exasperation. Matters are not very much improved when we come to the historian who qualifies all this by some such phrase as that 'Luther however was of an essentially mediæval cast of mind'; for this parenthetical homage to research is precisely the vice and the delusion of the whig historian, and this kind of afterthought only serves to show that he has not been placing things in their true context, but has been speaking of a modernised Luther in his narration of the story. But if one party is misconceived through this method of historical approach, it would seem that the opposing party is even more gravely maltreated. It is taken to have contributed nothing to the making of the present-day, and rather to have formed an obstruction; it cannot by the process of direct reference be shown to have stood as a root or a foreshadowing of the present; at worst it is converted into a kind of dummy that acts as a better foil to the grand whig virtues; and so it is often denied that very effort of historical understanding which would have helped to correct the original fallacy. In all this we tend to undo by our process of abstraction and our method of organisation all the work which historical research is achieving in detail; and we are overlooking the first condition of historical enquiry, which is to recognise how much other ages differed from our own.

If Protestants and Catholics of the 16th century could return to look at the 20th century, they would equally deplore this strange mad modern world, and much as they fought one another there is little doubt that they would be united in opposition to us; and Luther would confess that he had been wrong and wicked if it was by his doing that this liberty, this anarchy had been let loose, while his enemies would be quick to say that this decline of religion was bound to be the result of a schism such as his. The issue between Protestants and Catholics in the 16th century was an issue of their world and not of our world, and we are being definitely unhistorical, we are forgetting that Protestantism and Catholicism have both had a long history since 1517, if we argue from a rash analogy that the one was fighting for something like our modern world while the other was trying to prevent its coming. Our most secular historians, and the ones who are most grateful for that 'process of secularisation,' that 'break-up of mediævalism,' of which so much has been traced to the Reformation, are inclined to write sometimes as though Protestantism in itself was somehow constituted to assist that process. It is easy to forget how much Luther was in rebellion against the secularisation of Church and society, how much the Reformation shares the psychology of religious revivals, and to what an extent Luther's rebellion against the Papacy helped to provoke that very fanaticism of the Counterreformation against which we love to see the Protestant virtues shine. And it is not easy to keep in mind how much the Protestantism that we think of to-day and the Catholicism of these later times have themselves been affected in turn, though in different ways, by the secularisation that has taken place in society and by the dissolution of mediæval ideals.

The truth is much more faithfully summarised if we forgo all analogies with the present, and, braving the indignation of the whig historian together with all the sophistries that he is master of, count Protestants and Catholics of the 16th century as distant and strange people – as they really were – whose quarrels are as unrelated to ourselves as the factions of Blues and Greens in ancient Constantinople. In other words, it is better to assume unlikeness at first and let any likenesses that subsequently appear take their proper proportions in their proper context; just as in understanding an American it is wrong to assume first that he is like an Englishman and then quarrel with him for his unlikenesses, but much better to start with him as a foreigner and so see his very similarities with ourselves in a different light. Taking this view we shall see in the 16th century the clash of two forms of religion which in those days could not know how to be anything but intolerant; and from this clash we shall see emerging by more complicated paths than we should assume, indeed by paths almost too intricate to trace, some of our religious liberty, perhaps some of our religious indifference, and that whole tendency which the historian likes to call the process of secularisation. We shall see

Protestant and Catholic of the 16th century more like one another and more unlike ourselves than we have often cared to imagine — each claiming that his was the one true religion upon which both church and society should exclusively be established. We shall see that it was in fact precisely because they were so similar, in the exclusiveness of their claims, that they presented the world with one of the most fertile problems it has ever had to face. They presented the world with the fact which, though all men sought to close their eyes to it, ultimately proved inescapable — the co-existence of two forms of religion in one society; and they presented the world with the problem of how to make life possible and bearable in the face of such an unprecedented anomaly. Neither Protestant nor Catholic but precisely the fact that there were the two parties is the starting-point of the developments which took place.

It is here that we reach the second fault in the whig method of approach; for by its over-dramatisation of the story it tends to divert our attention from what is the real historical process. The whig historian too easily refers

changes and achievements to this party or that
personage, reading the issue as a purpose that
has been attaine , when very often it is a purpose that has been marred.   He gives an
over-simplification of the historical process.
The whig historian is fond of showing how
much Calvinism has contributed to the
development of modern liberty.   It is easy to
forget that in Geneva and in New England,
where Calvinism founded its New Jerusalem,
and so to speak had the field to itself, and was
in a position to have its own way with men,
the result was by no means entirely corrobora-
tive of all that is assumed in the whig thesis.
Whether our subject is Calvinism or anything
else, it is often easy to state practically the
converse of what the whig historian too readily
believes; and instead of being grateful to
Calvinism for our liberty we are just as reason-
able if we transfer our gratitude to those
conjunctures and accompanying circumstances
which in certain countries turned even Calvinism, perhaps in spite of itself, into the ally of
liberty.   By all means let us be grateful for
the Puritans of 17th century England, but let
us be grateful that they were for so long in a

minority and against the government; for this was the very condition of their utility.

There is a common error into which the whig historian is bound to fall as a result of his misconceptions concerning the historical process. He is apt to imagine the British constitution as coming down to us by virtue of the work of long generations of whigs and in spite of the obstructions of a long line of tyrants and tories. In reality it is the result of the continual interplay and perpetual collision of the two. It is the very embodiment of all the balances and compromises and adjustments that were necessitated by this interplay. The whig historian is apt to imagine the British constitution as coming down to us safely at last, in spite of so many vicissitudes; when in reality it is the result of those very vicissitudes of which he seems to complain. If there had never been a danger to our constitution there never would have been a constitution to be in danger. In the most concrete sense of the words our constitution is not merely the work of men and parties; it is the product of history. Now there is a sense in which the whig historian

sometimes seems to believe that there is an
unfolding logic in history, a logic which is on
the side of the whigs and which makes them
appear as co-operators with progress itself;
but there is a concrete sense in which it might
be said that he does not believe there is an
historical process at all. He does not see whig
and tory combining in virtue of their very
antagonism to produce those interactions
which turn one age into another. He does not
see that time is so to speak having a hand in the
game, and the historical process itself is working upon the pattern which events are taking.
He does not see the solidity with which
history is actually embodied in the British
constitution and similarly in the modern world.
He points out all the things which would never
have happened if Luther had not raised the
standard of the Reformation; and he does not
realise the fundamental fallacy that is involved
when this is inverted and all these things are
counted as the work and achievement of
Luther himself. In reality they are the result
of interaction; they are precipitated by complex history.

The consequences of his fundamental

misconception are never more apparent than
in the whig historian's quest for origins; for
we are subject to great confusion if we turn
this quest into a search for analogies, or if we
attempt to go too directly to look for the
present in the past. The very form of our
question is at fault if we ask, To whom do
we owe our religious liberty ? We may ask
how this liberty arose, but even then it takes
all history to give us the answer. We are in
error if we imagine that we have found the
origin of this liberty when we have merely
discovered the first man who talked about it.
We are wrong if we study the question in that
over-simplified realm which we call 'the
history of ideas,' or if we personify ideas in
themselves and regard them as self-standing
agencies in history. We are the victims of our
own phraseology if we think that we mean very
much when we say that religious liberty 'can
be traced back to' some person or other. And
if we assert that 'but for Luther' this liberty
would never have come down to us as it did
come, meaning to suggest that it has come
down to us as the glory and the achievement
of Luther, we are using a trick in text-book

terminology which has become the whig
historian's sleight-of-hand.   It may be true to
assert that there are many things in history
and in the present day which would never
have happened in the way they have happened
if Martin Luther had not defied a Pope; there
are equally many things which would not have
taken place as they have done if Columbus had
not discovered America; but it is as fallacious
to ascribe paternity to Luther in the one case
as it is to make Columbus responsible for
modern America; we can only say that both
men added a conditioning circumstance to a
whole network of other conditioning circumstances more than four centuries ago.   In
reality we can no more work out what religious
liberty owes to Luther than we can calculate
what proportion of the price of a man's suit
in 1930 ought to be divided between the
inventor of the spinning-jenny, the inventor
of the steam-engine, and the firm which
actually wove the cloth.   It is meaningless to
trace liberty along a line which goes back to
Luther merely because Luther at one time and
in a world of different connotations put forward some principles of freedom, from which

as a matter of fact he shrank when he saw some of the consequences that we see in them. It is not by a line but by a labyrinthine piece of network that one would have to make the diagram of the course by which religious liberty has come down to us, for this liberty comes by devious tracks and is born of strange conjunctures, it represents purposes marred perhaps more than purposes achieved, and it owes more than we can tell to many agencies that had little to do with either religion or liberty. We cannot tell to whom we must be grateful for this religious liberty and there is no logic in being grateful to anybody or anything except to the whole past which produced the whole present; unless indeed we choose to be grateful to that providence which turned so many conjunctures to our ultimate profit.

If we see in each generation the conflict of the future against the past, the fight of what might be called progressive versus reactionary, we shall find ourselves organising the historical story upon what is really an unfolding principle of progress, and our eyes will be fixed upon certain people who appear as the special agencies of that progress. We shall be tempted to ask the fatal question, To whom do we owe our religious liberty? But if we see in each generation a clash of wills out of which there emerges something that probably no man ever willed, our minds become concentrated upon the process that produced such an unpredictable issue, and we are more open for an intensive study of the motions and interactions that underlie historical change. In these circumstances the question will be stated in its proper form: How did religious liberty arise? The process of the historical transition will then be recognised to be unlike what the whig historian seems to assume — much less like the procedure of a logical argument and perhaps much more like the method by which a man can be imagined to work his way out of a 'complex.' It is a process which moves by mediations and those mediations may be provided by anything in the world — by men's sins or misapprehensions or by what we can only call fortunate conjunctures. Very strange bridges are used to make the passage from one state of things to another; we may lose sight of them in our surveys of general history, but their discovery is the glory of historical research. History is not the study of origins; rather it is the analysis of all the mediations by which the past was turned into our present.

Luther, precisely because he so completely assumed that the lay prince would be a godly prince, precisely because he so completely shared the assumptions of mediæval society, attributed to rulers some of the powers of Old Testament monarchs, and impressed upon them the duty of reforming the church. He was so sure that the ruler should be the servant of religion that he forgot the necessity of those safeguardings upon which the Papacy insisted in its dealings with temporal powers, and by calling rulers to his help at that particular moment he did something that helped kings and princes to become lords of everything and even masters of the church. If the Middle Ages had an inhibition against the control of spiritual matters by secular princes, Luther himself, at bottom, shared that inhibition to the utmost. Yet unawares and without liberating his own mind he helped — how much or how little would be too intricate for the historian to trace — to short-circuit the

mediæval argument and dissolve the complex that his generation laboured under. Yet
perhaps he did not do even so much as this;
perhaps at any other period his course of
action would have had no such result; for
kings in other ages had stepped in to reform
the church without gaining dominion over it.
Perhaps there was some still deeper movement in the time which was turning everything to the advantage of the lay prince and
the secular state, taking this and anything
else as a bridge to its own end. All the same
it is by intricate mediations such as this that
the religious society of the Middle Ages came
ultimately to transform itself into the secular
society of modern times; and it is important
to realise that such a transition as this process
of secularisation is one that could only come by
mediation, by the subtle removal of what were
complexes and inhibitions. It implied in
men's minds deep changes that could not have
been reached by logical argument, and it
implied in the world a whole series of movements that could not have been made by a
mighty volition. It implied new ideas that
could only come through the quiet dissolving

of prejudices, through the influence of new conditions that give rise to new prepossessions, through sundry pieces of forgetfulness in the handing of a tradition from one generation to another, and through many a process of elision by which men can slide into new points of view without knowing it. It implied the overthrow of Martin Luther's idea of the religious society, the destruction of the Calvinist's New Jerusalem, and the dissolution of the Mediæval and Papal ideal; it represented the history-making that was going on over men's heads, at cross-purposes with all of them. It is well that our minds should be focused upon that historical process which so cheats men of their purposes – that providence which deflects their labours to such unpredictable results. But the whig historian, driven to his last ditch, will still ascribe everything to Martin Luther. It is part of his verbal technique to make it still an added virtue in Luther that he worked for purposes greater than those of which he was conscious; as though the same were not true of the enemies of Luther, and equally true for that matter in the case of every one of us. The whig historian is interested in discovering agency in history, even where in this way he must avow it only implicit. . It is characteristic of his method that he should be interested in the agency rather than in the process. And this is how he achieves his simplification.

When the large map of the centuries is being traced out and the mind sweeps over broad ranges of abridged history, the whig fallacies become our particular snare, for they might have been invented to facilitate generalisation. The complexity of interactions can be telescoped till a movement comes to appear as a simple progression. It is all the more easy to impute historical change to some palpable and direct agency. What we call 'causes' are made to operate with astonishing immediacy. So it is when we are forming our general surveys, when we are placing the Reformation in the whole scheme of history, that we project our wider whig interpretations and draw our diagram in the strongest lines. In regard to the Reformation it might be said that the whig fallacies of secular historians have had a greater effect over a wider field than any theological bias that can be imputed to Protestant writers. And the tendency is to magnify the Reformation even when it is not entirely complimentary to the Protestants to do so. It is easy to be dramatic and see Luther as something like a rebel against mediævalism. It is pleasant to make him responsible for religious toleration and freedom of thought. It is tempting to bring his whole movement into relief by showing how it promoted the rise of the secular state, or to say with one of our writers that without Martin Luther there would have been no Louis XIV. It may even be plausible to claim that Protestantism contributed to the rise of the capitalist; that in its ethics were evolved the more than seven deadly virtues which have helped to provide the conditions for an industrial civilisation; and then to bring this to a climax in the statement: 'Capitalism is the social counterpart of Calvinist Theology.' So we complete the circle and see Protestantism behind modern society, and we further another optical illusion — that history is divided by great watersheds of which the Reformation is one. Sometimes it would seem that we regard Protestantism as a Thing, a fixed and definite

object that came into existence in 1517; and
we seize upon it as a source, a cause, an origin,
even of movements that were taking place
concurrently; and we do this with an air of
finality, as though Protestantism itself had
no antecedents, as though it were a fallacy to
go behind the great watershed, as though
indeed it would blunt the edge of our story to
admit the workings of a process instead of
assuming the interposition of some direct
agency. It is all an example of the fact that
for the compilation of trenchant history there
is nothing like being content with half the
truth. We gain emphasis and at the same
time we magnify the whig interpretation of
history by stopping the enquiry into the
historical process at the precise point where
our own discoveries have made it interesting.
In this way we are able to take the whig short
cut to absolute judgments that seem astonish-
ingly self-evident.

It seems possible to say that if we are seeking to discover how the mediæval world was
changed into the world that we know, we
must go behind Protestantism and the Reformation to a deeper tide in the affairs of men,

to a movement which we may indeed discern but can scarcely dogmatise about, and to a prevailing current, which, though we must never discover it too soon, is perhaps the last thing we can learn in our research upon the historical process. It does seem for example that before the Reformation some wind in the world had clearly set itself to play on the side of kings, and in many a country a hundred weather-vanes, on steeple and on mansion, on college and on court, had turned before the current to show that the day of monarchy had come. And indeed some little detail in popular psychology would seem to have shown the way of the wind as clearly as some of the larger developments in the constitutional machinery of a state. Further it is possible to say that when there is such a tide in the affairs of men, it may use any channel to take it to its goal — it may give any other movement a turn in its own direction. For some reason Renaissance and Reformation and rising Capitalism were made to work to the glory of kings. And even if in their origin these movements had been rather of a contrary tenor — even though a religious awakening might not in itself seem likely to

increase the power of secular monarchs over
the church — still the deeper drift might carry
with it the surface currents, and sweep them in
to swell the prevailing tide.   Perhaps — to
take one example — it was because the princes
were already growing both in power and in
self-assertion that the Reformation was drawn
into an alliance with them, which had so great
influence on Protestants as well as Kings.

The large process which turned the mediæval world into the modern world, the process
which transformed the religious society into
the secular state of modern times, was wider
and deeper and stronger than the Reformation
itself.   The Reformation may have been
something more than merely a symptom or a
result of such a process, and we should be
assuming too much if we said that it was only
an incident in the transition.   But the historian
would be very dogmatic who insisted on
regarding it as a cause.   Protestantism was the
subject of rapid historical change from the
very moment of its birth.   It was quickly
transformed into something which its original
leaders would scarcely have recognised.   And
though it might be true to say that later

Protestants were only working out the implications of the original movement, the fact remains that they worked them out in a certain direction; they found implications that Luther did not intend and would not have liked; and it was precisely in this turn that Protestantism acquired the associations that have become so familiar, the ones which are roughly denoted by the words, Individualism, Capitalism, and the Secular State. Precisely where the whig historian ascribes influence, the Reformation itself most obviously came under the influence of the tendencies of the times. If the movement had political, economic, or sociological consequences, this was because it had itself become entangled in forces that seemed almost inescapable, and if it gave them leverage this was because it had itself become subject to their workings. It is not sufficient to imply that Protestantism was in any way responsible for the capitalist; it is not sufficient to see that the religious and economic realms were reacting on one another; we must be prepared to watch the truth of history water down into a banality, and allow that to some degree

Protestants and capitalists were being carried in the same direction by the same tide. If Roman Catholicism proved less amenable, this was not simply because it was an older and more hardened system, but because the remarkably assimilative mediæval Catholic church had become the remarkably unassimilative modern Roman Catholic one, as though the Lutheran movement had turned it in upon itself, and had set it in opposition to innovation, even to the deeper tendencies of the age. Further it is possible to say, or at least we must leave room for saying – we must not by our mere organisation of the historical story close the door against it – that the Reformation in its original character as a reassertion of religious authority and a regeneration of the religious society was in some sense an actual protest against that comprehensive movement which was changing the face of the world; but that being the subject of rapid historical change from the very start it came itself under the influence of that movement, and was turned into the ally of some of the very tendencies which it had been born to resist.

The watershed is broken down if we place

the Reformation in its historical context and if
we adopt the point of view which regards
Protestantism itself as the product of history.
But here greater dangers lurk and we are
bordering on heresy more blasphemous than
that of the whigs, for we may fall into the
opposite fallacy and say that the Reformation
did nothing at all. If there is a deeper tide
that rolls below the very growth of Protestantism nothing could be more shallow than
the history which is mere philosophising
upon such a movement, or even the history
which discovers it too soon. And nothing
could be more hasty than to regard it as a self-
standing, self-determined agency behind history, working to its purpose irrespective of the
actual drama of events. It might be used to
show that the Reformation made no difference
in the world, that Martin Luther did not
matter, and that the course of the ages is unaffected by anything that may happen; but
even if this were true the historian would not
be competent to say so, and in any case such
a doctrine would be the very negation of
history. It would be the doctrine that the
whole realm of historical events is of no

significance whatever. It would be the converse of the whig over-dramatisation. The deep movement that is in question does not explain everything, or anything at all. It does not exist apart from historical events and cannot be disentangled from them. Perhaps there is nothing the historian can do about it, except to know that it is there. One fallacy is to be avoided, and once again it is the converse of that of the whigs. If the Reformation is not merely a 'cause,' at the same time we cannot say that it is merely a 'result.' It is like the mind of a human being: though we find the historical antecedents of everything in it, still, in our capacity as historians at least, we cannot deny that something different is produced. In this sense we may say that history is the study not of origins but of mediations, but it is the study of effective mediations genuinely leading from something old to something which the historian must regard as new. It is essentially the study of transition, and to the historian the only absolute is change.

There were many reasons why the Reformation should have provided a countless number of interesting forms of this kind of mediation.

Merely by creating an upheaval in the 16th century it threw a great many questions into the melting-pot. By the very intensity of the warfare and controversy it caused it must have hastened the decision of many conflicts of forces and ideas. By the novel situations it created and the unsettlement it produced, it must have given special opening for many new combinations of ideas. And the mere fact that there were such overturns in society, necessitating so much reorganisation, must have prevented in many countries the solid resistance of stable and established institutions to whatever tendencies existed in the times. For all these reasons and for many others the Reformation is the most interesting example one could find for the study of the mediations by which one age is turned into another – for the examination of an historical transition. We can see why the Reformation may have been something more than a passenger, and may have been an ally, giving actual leverage to forces that we may regard as existing already. And the result will be different from whig history because there will be less of that subtle implication that the changes of the 16th

century can be accounted for by reference to
the nature or essence of Protestantism. There
will be more room left for such comments on
this whole period of transition, as that the
Reformation, by the mere fact that it produced
upheaval, was bound to make transformations
more rapid in every sphere of life. And if it is
said that on this argument the Reformation
still does nothing more than leave the field
open for the play of those forces which were
already at work, and so serves merely as a
hindrance of hindrances – if we must go
further and admit that we are not in a position
to deny the genius and personal achievement
of a man like Martin Luther – here we may
agree with the whig historian, we may even
say that the Reformation in a certain sense
brings something new into history; but even
here there is a subtle difference. We could
not imagine Luther as having produced
something out of nothing; it lies in the very
terms of our study of history that we should
discover the historical antecedents of everything that Luther said or did; he would still
be himself an example of historical mediation,
performing what is really a work of transition,

carrying what was old into something which we could agree to be genuinely new. And it might be suggested that if history is approached in this way – not as a question of origins but as a question of transitions, not as the subject of 'causes' but as the subject of 'mediations' – historical interpretation would become less whig and change would seem less cataclysmic. History would lose some of the paradoxes, such as those which are at least implied in the statement : 'Capitalism is the social counterpart of Calvinist Theology'; and the world of the historian would become much more like the world as it appears in life. In reality this method of approach would tend to lead us to the view that the Reformation was essentially a religious movement, as it must have appeared to its original leaders. We should discover that if so much of the modern world has been placed on the shoulders of Luther, this has been due at least in part to the historian's optical illusion, to certain features in the technique of history-writing, and to the exploitation of that dubious phraseology which has become the historian's stock-in-trade. We should end by being at least more prepared to recognise that in history as in life Luther must stand or fall on his genius and his genuineness as a religious leader. And if the Reformation had economic or political consequences we should be more ready to see that this was because it became entangled in tendencies which were already in existence, and which indeed it does not seem to have altered or deflected so greatly as is sometimes assumed.

Finally in criticism of the whig historian who studies the past with too direct reference to the present day, it may be said that his method of procedure actually defeats his original confessed purpose which was to use the past for the elucidation of the present. If we look for things in the course of history only because we have found them already in the world of to-day, if we seize upon those things in the 16th century which are most analogous to what we know in the 20th, the upshot of all our history is only to send us back finally to the place where we began, and to ratify whatever conceptions we originally had in regard to our own times. It makes all the difference in the world whether we already assume the present at the beginning of our study of history and keep it as a basis of reference, or whether we wait and suspend our judgment until we discover it at the end. The controversialists of the 17th century who made a too direct reference of Magna Carta to their own day, were not using the past in such a way as to give them better insight into their own generation, but were arguing in a circle, and, perhaps happily for them, were making their history confirm some of their misconceptions concerning their own present. If we turn our present into an absolute to which all other generations are merely relative, we are in any case losing the truer vision of ourselves which history is able to give; we fail to realise those things in which we too are merely relative, and we lose a chance of discovering where, in the stream of the centuries, we ourselves, and our ideas and prejudices, stand. In other words we fail to see how we ourselves are, in our turn, not quite autonomous or unconditioned, but a part of the great historical process; not pioneers merely, but also passengers in the movement of things.

IV. HISTORY AND JUDGMENTS OF VALUE

HISTORY has been taken out of the hands of the strolling minstrels and the pedlars of stories and has been accepted as a means by which we can gain more understanding of ourselves and our place in the sun – a more clear consciousness of what we are tending to and what we are trying to do. It would seem even that we have perhaps placed too much faith in the study of this aspect of ourselves, and that we have let our thinking run to history with more enthusiasm than judgment. The historian like every other specialist is quick to over-step the bounds of his subject and elicit from history more than history can really give; and he is for ever tempted to bring his stories to a conclusiveness and his judgments to a finality that are not warranted by either the materials or the processes of his research. Behind all the fallacies of the whig historian there lies the passionate desire to come to a judgment of values, to make history

answer questions and decide issues and to give
the historian the last word in a controversy.
He imagines that he is inconclusive unless he
can give a verdict; and studying Protestant
and Catholic in the 16th century he feels that
loose threads are still left hanging unless he
can show which party was in the right. He
wishes to come to a general proposition, that
can be held as a truth demonstrated by
history, a lesson that can be taken away and
pondered apart from the accidents of a
particular historical episode; and unless he can
attain to something like this he feels that he
has been working at a sum which had no answer, he has been wasting himself upon mere
processes, he has been watching complication and change for the mere sake of complication and change. Yet this, which he seems
to disparage, is precisely the function of the
historian. The eliciting of general truths or of
propositions claiming universal validity is the
one kind of consummation which it is beyond
the competence of history to achieve.

The historian is concerned with the concrete and is at home in the world of facts and
people and happenings. The web spun out

of the play of time and circumstance is everything to him.   Accidents and conjunctures
and curious juxtapositions of events are the
very stuff of his story.   All his art is to recapture a moment and seize upon particulars
and fasten down a contingency.   The theorist
who loves principles for themselves may discuss them freely, for he discusses them so to
speak in the air; but the historian must bring
them to earth for he only studies them in other
men's lives; he must see principles caught
amongst chance and accident; he must watch
their logic being tricked and entangled in the
events of a concrete world.   The historian is
essentially the observer, watching the moving
scene.   Like the traveller he describes an un-
known country to us who cannot visit it; and
like the traveller he deals with the tangible,
the concrete, the particular; he is not greatly
concerned with philosophy or abstract reasoning.   Were he too much a philosopher he
would be perhaps too impatient of the waste
and repetitiveness and triviality of all the
things that it is his business to notice, and
perhaps like Thomas Carlyle he would im-
print too much of his own mind upon the

shape of events. History indeed is a form of descriptive writing as books of travel are. It is concerned with the processes of life rather than with the meaning or purpose or goal of life. It is interested in the way in which ideals move men and give a turn to events rather than in the ultimate validity of the ideals themselves. One might say that rather than being interested in light and the nature of light, the historian studies merely its refractions as it breaks up in the external world — he is concerned to examine colours, he is interested in a whole universe of colour. His training and habits of mind and all the methods of his research fasten him down to the particular and the concrete and make him essentially an observer of the events of the external world. For this cause it has generally happened that historians have reflected little upon the nature of things and even the nature of their own subject, and have indeed what they feel to be a healthy kind of distrust of such disembodied reasoning. They have been content as a rule to accept current views of the place of history in the scheme of knowledge, to apply a hasty common sense to the problems that arise and to make rather facile analogies from the other arts and sciences. They have critically examined and placed upon a scientific basis only one aspect of their study, and that the concrete side – the use of sources and the weighing of evidence – and they have not been so careful in the establishment of a system in regard to their organisation of a historical story, or in regard to their processes of inference upon their subject. They are not happy when they leave the concrete world and start reasoning in a general way.

The value of history lies in the richness of its recovery of the concrete life of the past. It is a story that cannot be told in dry lines, and its meaning cannot be conveyed in a species of geometry. There is not an essence of history that can be got by evaporating the human and the personal factors, the incidental or momentary or local things, and the circumstantial elements, as though at the bottom of the well there were something absolute, some truth independent of time and circumstance. There may be an essence of Protestantism and a formula that lies at the root of the matter, but there is no essence of the history of the

Reformation, no formula that can take the place of the whole story. When he describes the past the historian has to recapture the richness of the moments, the humanity of the men, the setting of external circumstances, and the implications of events ; and far from sweeping them away, he piles up the concrete, the particular, the personal; for he studies the changes of things which change and not the permanence of the mountains and the stars. To recover the personality of Martin Luther in a full rich concrete sense — including of course all that some people might consider to be the accidents and non-essentials — is not only the aim of the historian, but is an end in itself; and here the thing which is un-historical is to imagine that we can get the essence apart from the accidents; it is to think of Luther in terms of a formula, 'the founder of Protestantism,' 'the apostle of religious liberty.' The whole process of historical study is a movement towards historical research — it is to carry us from the general to the particular, from the abstract to the concrete, from the thesis that the Reformation led to liberty to an actual vision of all the chances and

changes which brought about the modern
world.

The fourth century of the Christian era, for
example, represents an age when important
things were happening, and paganism com-
pleted its decline, while Christianity entered
upon its victory. It is obvious that great
and palpable human issues were being raised
and decided in these years, and special
varieties of human relationship arose, giving
life and experience a peculiar intensity. One
cannot avoid asking what men were like when
they were breaking with an old order of things,
changing Gods and putting on new habits
and making new adjustments to life. It must
be interesting to learn how such a human
crisis would present itself in a single soul, in a
home, a village, a city, a court. What did men
think of an emperor who accepted the guid-
ance and even the reproof of bishops, and
refused to grant state-aid for the service of
the ancient gods ? What kind of *rapproche-
ments* took place between declining paganism
and rising Christianity ? What did the
Christians borrow from pagan rites and fêtes
and ideas – what consciously and what

unawares ? What was the feeling of the old men when the young were forgetting their gods, and in the after-day, when evil fell, did not some men take their Christianity with a misgiving ? It is easy to see the fight between Christianity and Paganism as a play of forces and to discuss it so to speak in the abstract; but much more illuminating to watch it as the interplay of personalities and people, with the four winds of heaven blowing around them; much more interesting if we can take the general statement with which we began, the mere formula for what happened in this age, and pursue it in its concrete incidence till we discover into what manifold detail it differentiates itself, and learn how various were its workings in actual life, how surprising even its by-play and the side-issues which it raised, how rich its underlying complexity and its implications in human story. It is along this road that the historian carries us, away from the world of general ideas.

It is not for him to give a philosophical explanation of what happens in time and space. Indeed any history that he writes ought to be as capable of varied philosophical

interpretation as life itself seems to be.   In the
last resort the historian's explanation of what
has happened is not a piece of general reasoning at all.   He explains the French Revolution
by discovering exactly what it was that
occurred; and if at any point we need further
elucidation all that he can do is to take us into
greater detail, and make us see in still more
definite concreteness what really did take
place.   In doing this he is bound to lead us to
something which we never could have inferred.
And this is his justification; it is the romance
of historical research.   We, after a survey
of the Reformation, may seek to deduce from
general principles what must have been the
reasons for its occurrence; but there is all
the difference in the world between this kind
of philosophising and a close and concrete
examination of how Martin Luther's great
decisions came to be made.   This accounts for
the air of unreality which hangs around much
of our general history when it has been compiled with too great impatience of historical
research.   The result of historical study is
precisely the demonstration of the fallacy of
our arm-chair logic – the proof of the poverty

of all this kind of speculation when compared with the surprise of what actually did take place. And the historian's passion for manuscripts and sources is not the desire to confirm facts and dates or to correct occasional points of error in the historical story, but the desire to bring himself into genuine relationship with the actual, with all the particularities of chance and change – the desire to see at first-hand how an important decision comes to be made. So the last word of the historian is not some fine firm general statement; it is a piece of detailed research. It is a study of the complexity that underlies any generalisation that we can make.

Above all it is not the rôle of the historian to come to what might be called judgments of value. He may try to show how men came to differ in religion, but he can no more adjudicate between religions than he can adjudicate between systems of philosophy; and though he might show that one religion has been more favourable in its sociological consequences than another, though even – which is much more difficult – he might think he has shown that the one is bound to be better in its ultimate consequences through time – still it is not for him to beg the question of the assessment of material losses against what might be considered spiritual and eternal gains. His rôle is to describe; he stands impartial between Christian and Mohammedan; he is interested in neither one religion nor the other except as they are entangled in human lives. Though he might describe, if he can untwist them, the economic consequences of the Inquisition in modern Spain, though he might even show that the Inquisition was in some way responsible for reducing Spain from the ranks of the great powers, still he has not shown that it was fatal to happiness, and he cannot beg questions concerning what is the good life. At the end of it all the Spaniard might retort that the Inquisition which robbed him of greatness was the institution which once gave him prestige and power; and it is proper that the historian should be driven to pursue his enquiries a step further, and ask why the Inquisition which in one set of circumstances helped the power of Spain should in another set of circumstances have contributed to its downfall. He is back in his proper place when he takes us away from simple and absolute judgments and by returning to the historical context entangles everything up again. He is back in his proper place when he tells us that a thing is good or harmful according to circumstances, according to the interactions that are produced. If history can do anything it is to remind us of those complications that undermine our certainties, and to show us that all our judgments are merely relative to time and circumstance.

There is one argument against the whig interpretation of history which is paradoxical and is in conflict with all our habits of mind, for it takes away what many might feel to be the virtue and the utility of history, and it robs the historian of his most trenchant attitudes and his grandest note of finality. It lies in the fact that we can never assert that history has proved any man right in the long run. We can never say that the ultimate issue, the succeeding course of events, or the lapse of time have proved that Luther was right against the Pope or that Pitt was wrong against Charles James Fox. We cannot say that the ultimate consequences of Luther's action have justified his purposes or his conduct; for the

modern secularised world has no more vindicated Luther's mastering purpose or his ideal
of a religious society than it vindicates the
mediæval ideal of the Popes; and in any case
we cannot work out the ultimate consequences
of Luther's conduct unless we wish to imitate
the schoolboy who, writing on the results of
Columbus's discovery of America, enumer-
ated amongst other things the execution of
Charles I, the war of the Spanish Succession
and the French Revolution. By great labour
we can perhaps track down the displacements which the Lutheran revolt produced in
Luther's own day; we may be able to disentangle something roughly like causes and
effects in the transition from one generation
to the next; but very soon we can trace out
nothing more, we can only see the results of
Luther's conduct entangled with the results of
everything else that was producing change at
that period; we can only focus ourselves upon
the new situation as a whole and watch fresh
displacements being produced now by fresh
conjunctures. The most that we can say is
that if Luther did ill in his day, the evil for
which he was responsible was part of the

situation that men in future had to face; and
that his successors, working upon the new state
of the problem, would set their purposes anew
and still make all things work together for
good, though henceforward it might have to
be some new good that they set their hearts
upon.   When the sins and errors of an age
have made the world impossible to live in, the
next generation, seeking to make life tolerable
again, may be able to find no way save by the
surrender of cherished ideals, and so may find
themselves compelled to cast about for new
dreams and purposes.   An important aspect
of the historical process is the work of the new
generation for ever playing providence over
even the disasters of the old, and being driven
to something like a creative act for the very
reason that life on the old terms has become
impossible.   It represents a complication that
may be hidden from our sight if the story is
telescoped into a whig version of abridged
history.   For this reason we have to be on our
guard when the whig historian tells us for
example that the Reformation is justified
because it led ultimately to liberty; we must
avoid the temptation to make what seem to

be the obvious inferences from this statement;
for it is possible to argue against the whig
historian that the ultimate issue which he
applauds only came in the long run from the
fact that, in its immediate results, the Reformation was so disastrous to liberty.

The Reformation which is so often regarded
as a result and continuation of the Renaissance
– a parallel movement of man's expanding
mind – might also be looked upon as a re-
assertion of religious authority in the world, a
revolt against the secularisation, the laxness
and the sins of the time. Luther, who appeals
to us so strongly as an innovator and a rebel
against constituted authority, was behind
everything else the religious leader, in a sense
the revivalist, whose rebellion was only an
incident in his great attempt to establish right
religion in the world. Luther and Calvin were
both alike in that they attacked the papal and
mediæval conception of the religious society;
but it is doubtful whether the Biblical Com-
monwealth for which they laboured would
have been any less severe in its control of the
individual, or would have commended itself
to these men if it had been less severe. And

although the Bible has proved to be the most flexible of authorities and the most capable of progressive interpretation, it has yet to be demonstrated that the Reformers who used it to confound the Popes did not regard it as a more firm and rigid authority than the Roman tradition or the canon-law, of which they seem to have condemned precisely the innovations and the development. Luther, when he was making his development of religious doctrine, was not hindered but was generously encouraged by his superiors in the Catholic Church, and he was not molested when, like so many other preachers of his day, he fulminated in his sermons against the common attitude to indulgences. One might say that the very action which precipitated the break with Rome was prompted by Luther's own intolerance of what he deemed wrong religion in other people. It might be argued that what Luther rebelled against was not the severity but the laxity of the Popes.

In any case the 16th century was a time when any serious error concerning divine things was almost universally regarded as blasphemy; when the state and the secular rulers could not imagine that religious non-conformity might be consistent with public order; and when a great theological controversy was calculated to make religions militant and fanatical.   One might have predicted that in the 16th century a religious movement which assumed large proportions and implied a schism in the Catholic Church would almost make the continent run with blood; particularly if it provoked by reaction a revival of religious fanaticism in Rome itself.   It is difficult to escape the conclusion that Luther's break with the Papacy — for which the Popes themselves were so greatly responsible, since they seemed determined to drive him to revolt — had disastrous results in the succeeding generation and was terrible in its effects on life and society.   I do not know who could deny that the Reformation provoked a revival of religious passions, religious fanaticism and religious hatreds which were unlike the world to which things had seemed to be moving in the year 1500; and when we look at Erasmus and Machiavelli and the spirit of the Renaissance we must at least wonder whether freedom of thought and modern rationalism might not have had an easier course if Luther had never resuscitated militant religion. Even though it might be argued that the terrible wars which devastated so many countries during a whole century were not by any means solely due to their ostensible religious cause, it is none the less certain that religion contributed to them their fanaticism and intensity, and the introduction of the religious element neither helped to clarify the other issues, nor tended to make them more capable of compromise. It would be as great a mistake to deny the genuineness of religious fanaticism in this period, as to ascribe all the horrors and evils to the iniquity of Roman Catholics; for the real seat of the tragedy lay in the ideas which Luther and Calvin and the Popes held in common and held with equal intensity – the idea that society and government should be founded on the basis of the one authoritative religion, that all thought should be dominated by religion, and that within this religious society no heresy or blasphemy or abomination should be allowed to rear itself up in defiance of God. There is little point in blaming either Luther or the Popes for a view of religious authority which was connected with their fundamental assumptions concerning society, or in attacking them for a belief in persecution which was perhaps only the reflex side of their religious certainty; but we can say that when such assumptions were so deeply rooted in the minds of almost all religious men, a movement like the Reformation, working in direct antagonism to the hitherto recognised and constituted authority, was bound to be disastrous in its terrestrial consequences. Catholics were not alone responsible for the tragedy and the devastations of the religious struggles; we can only say that Catholics and Protestants alike, working upon assumptions which they held in common, produced by their clash, by their very co-existence in one society and in Christendom, wars and bitterness and disasters which are too terrible to contemplate.

If we focus our vision afresh and fix our attention on the post-Reformation world, we see a generation faced with a new weight of problems, and confronted particularly by the strange problem that arose out of the co-existence of two forms of religion in one society – what we should call the problem of religious minorities. We can see novel experiments being tried – a great attempt to make life possible and tolerable again; and it is almost amusing to see the measures to which men had to resort because they could not escape the fundamental assumption that church and society should be co-extensive – they could not imagine that a government should be anything but the first servant of the one true faith. A long road had to be taken before religion could be regarded as an optional matter for the individual, or churches could be accepted as voluntary societies within the state. Elizabeth of England tried to secure 'comprehension' by a *via media*, so that one inclusive religious organisation could cover the whole country. Catherine de' Medici, failing comprehension, was willing to tolerate a religious minority, somewhat as an anomaly, almost as a 'state within the state.' Toleration was enforced at times as a suspension of the problem, being regarded at first, very often, as an interim measure – an attempt to reach a *modus vivendi* until the healing of the church. Parties like that of the Politiques in France

might still acknowledge that persecution was
the religious ideal and one religion alone the
true one, but decided that persecution could
not be carried out on the scale of a massacre,
and said that the state must not be wrecked
for the sake of religion. As the struggles pro-
ceeded the state found the opportunity to rise
into the position of adjudicator, while the
religious bodies tended to look like conflicting
parties within the state; the secular government, instead of regarding itself as the servant
of the one true faith, might even stand out as
the guardian of the interests of society, im-
posing peace upon religious factions. In all
these ways toleration emerges with the return
of religious indifference. It comes as a secular
ideal. It is the re-assertion of the rights of
society and the rights of this world against
religions which by their warfare and by the
absoluteness of their claims were acting in
defiance of social consequences. Elizabeth of
England, Catherine de' Medici, William the
Silent, Wallenstein, and all those parties
which in one country or another adopted the
attitude of the Politiques, attempted to heal
the sorrows of the time and to overcome the

Reformation tragedy by subordinating religion
to policy. They helped the cause of liberty
because they were too worldly, and from the
point of view of their own age they were
perhaps too wicked, to support one religion or
another in defiance of social consequences, and
in disregard of a political good.

But all the time religious bodies themselves
were altering and were being affected by
changes in the world. From the first all
parties had cried out for freedom of conscience
against the dominating church; and each had
attacked the persecutions of the other; but
Protestants, arising as a minority in so many
countries, had the greater experience of this
manner of protesting. Some people were
bound ultimately to arrive at the view that all
persecution even on behalf of the truth was
wicked. The Bible became a more fluid and
flexible authority than Luther or Calvin had
imagined it to be. Protestantism broke up
into more divisions and parties than its original
leaders would have liked to see. These sects
could not for ever go on persecuting one
another when the Papacy menaced them all.
The Protestants were in a better position than

the Catholics to learn the relativity of the
various forms of religion, and to regard church
organisation as the subject of experiment, and
doctrine as the subject of enquiry. Protestants came to tolerate one another, though it
was long before most of them could tolerate a
Catholic. There emerged ideas like that of
the Independents in England, who advocated
a congregational system that permitted of
religious diversity within the state. Toleration, which had been a secular policy, a
political necessity, was turned into a religious
ideal; and churches came to take their place
as voluntary societies within the state. Instead
of the old ideal of the state as one uniform
and coherent religious society – the ideal of
Lutheran, Calvinist, Anabaptist, Anglican and
Roman Catholic – there grew up the principle
of religious liberty, the idea of the secular state
within which men could join any religious
group or choose not to belong to any at all,
the view that a government must be indifferent
to men's choice of church or religion. The
original Protestants had brought new passion
into the ideal of the state as a religious society
and they had set about to discipline this

society more strictly than ever upon the pattern of the Bible. The later Protestants reversed a fundamental purpose and became the allies of individualism and the secular state.

At the back of everything, moving men to this change of purpose, this revision of ideals, was the tragedy of the Reformation, the havoc caused by the co-existence of two forms of religion in the same society. It was because the results of the Reformation had been so disastrous to life and liberty that people were driven to re-examine their principles and were compelled even to alter religious ideals. The truth is that if in a certain generation men are bitterly quarrelling over the claims of one religion and another, the havoc may become so serious that the very state of the problem is changed, and men slide into a world of new issues and are diverted to new preoccupations. The question that exercises the next generation will be how to secure some sort of religious peace, how at least to contrive that religious controversy shall not spread ruin over the world. The whig historian assuming a false continuity in events, overlooks this shifting of the problem and ignores this transition

between one generation and another. He likes
to imagine religious liberty issuing beautifully out of Protestantism when in reality it
emerges painfully and grudgingly out of something quite different, out of the tragedy of the
post-Reformation world. He imagines that
Luther has been vindicated by the course of
subsequent events when in fact it was the
generations after Luther which performed the
work of reconciliation, it was the heritage of
disaster itself which drove men later to a
creative act. The whig historian thinks that
the course of history, the passage of centuries
can give judgment on a man or an age or a
movement. In reality there is only one thing
that history can say on this matter, and this
itself is so commonplace that it can almost be
reduced to a piece of tautology. It is, that
provided disaster is not utterly irretrievable —
provided a generation is not destroyed or a
state wiped entirely from the map — there is
no sin or error or calamity can take place but
succeeding generations will make the best of
it; and though it be a Black Death or a Fire
of London that comes as a scourge and a
visitation, men will still make virtue of

necessity and use the very downfall of the old
world as the opportunity for making a new,
till the whig historian looking back upon the
catastrophe can see only the acquired advan-
tages and the happy readjustments. So in the
result the whig historian will be tempted to
forget the sufferings of a generation, and will
find it easy to assert that the original tragedy
was no tragedy at all. We of the present-day
can be thankful for the religious quarrels of
the 16th century, as we are thankful for the
Black Death and the Fire of London — because
the very disasters drove men to what was
tantamount to a creative act; and we, coming
in the after-flow of the centuries, can see only
the good that was produced. But we are
deceived by the optical illusion if we deny that
when Luther rebelled against the Catholic
Church, and the Popes so deliberately hounded
him into rebellion, they did not between them
produce a tragedy which meant the sacrifice of
more than one generation.

V. THE ART OF THE HISTORIAN

It may be objected that the view of history which has been set up against the whig interpretation represents the dullest of all things, history without bias, the history that is partial to nobody. The mind that too greatly strives to be an open mind is on this argument striving only to be featureless. The historian writes under too many repressions if he is dominated only by the fear of saying something wrong. Perhaps it is true that impartiality is impossible, and the appearance of having achieved it is only the greatest of all illusions. Perhaps even if it could be attained the object itself is far from being desirable; for it would seem that the imagination could not take wing if history were a world in which our feelings were not involved. A work of history can indeed be a dull weight of dead matter and there have been historians who have seemed to do nothing more than transcribe their elaborate card-indexes — as though they themselves had no function to perform, no work of mediation to carry out between the subject-matter and the reader. It is easy to overlook or to misrepresent the contribution which the historian makes to our understanding of the past. It is easy to forget that in the art of the historian there is the exhilarating moment, the creative act. It is by no means the historian's duty to whittle himself down to a mere transparency, and simply to transcribe information with colourless, passionless impartiality.

It is through something like a creative act of the historical imagination that we have discovered how to reach some understanding of the Middle Ages, we have found a way of realising the terms upon which life was lived in those days, we have learned how to come with a different feeling for things and so to discern the inner relations of a world so different from our own. And we differ from the men of the Renaissance and the thinkers of the 18th century not merely in our conception of these mediæval days, but in the fact that we have made the actual effort of historical understanding, in the fact that we consider such an effort good and necessary. The historian is not merely the observer; for if he were this only he would be a poor observer. In a special sense he goes out to meet the past and his work is not merely the function of mind, it is a venture of the personality. This is why Sir Walter Scott has helped us to understand the Covenanters, and Thomas Carlyle has made an important contribution to our estimate of Cromwell. The historian is something more than the mere passive external spectator. Something more is necessary if only to enable him to seize the significant detail and discern the sympathies between events and find the facts that hang together. By imaginative sympathy he makes the past intelligible to the present. He translates its conditioning circumstances into terms which we to-day can understand. It is in this sense that history must always be written from the point of view of the present. It is in this sense that every age will have to write its history over again.

There is a kind of awareness that only comes through insight and sympathy and imagination, and is perhaps absent from us when we are too alert for a purely scientific end. It is absent from us if we read our documents only literally, and miss their innuendo because we lack the historic sense. Something of this awareness is necessary to catch the overtones in history and in life, to read between the lines and touch the human side of our subject, for which our minds may be too mathematical if mind does not work along with sympathy and imagination. It will always be something of an art to understand the ways of our next-door neighbour, and however learned we may be in psychology something like divination will be necessary before we can see its bearings upon any particular human being. Impartiality in a historian stands condemned if it means the intellect in a state of indifference and every passion at rest. We go to the past to discover not facts only but significances. It is necessary that we should go with instinct and sympathy alive and all our humanity awake. It is necessary that we should call up from the resources of our nature all the things which deflect the thought of the scientist but combine to enrich the poet's.

It cannot be denied that the whig historian has performed this part of his function admirably, but he has done it for what might be described as only one side of the historical story. His own assumptions have on many occasions given him the incentive to seek historical understanding; his own view of the course of history has provided him with those sympathies that waken imagination; the theses he has been inclined to defend have driven him to ingenuity, and he has learned to put himself in another man's place and to think himself into the conditioning circumstances that governed other men's lives. The whig historian is an example of the emotional drive that is necessary to make us question conclusions that seem foregone. He is an example of the fact that prejudice and passion itself can make a contribution to historical understanding. But it has happened that Protestants have been able to search their minds for a defence and an understanding of the persecution that Luther favoured, and have not realised that the very arguments they were using were part of the armoury of defence which Papal persecution has had at its command. The case against the whig historian lies in the fact that he brings the effort of understanding to a halt. He stops the work of imaginative sympathy at a point that could almost be fixed by a formula. It would not be untrue to say that, apart from specialist work of recent date, much greater ingenuity and a much higher imaginative endeavour have been brought into play upon the whigs, progressives and even revolutionaries of the past, than have been exercised upon the elucidation of tories and conservatives and reactionaries. The whig historian withdraws the effort in the case of the men who are most in need of it.

History would be for ever unsatisfying if it did not cast a wider net for the truth; for if in one aspect it is the study of change, in another aspect it is the study of diversity. The historian like the novelist is bound to be glad that it takes all sorts of men to make a world. Like the novelist he can regret only one kind – the complete bore – and take care not to describe him with too great verisimilitude. For the rest, all is grist to his mill. His greatest limitation would be a defect of imaginative sympathy, whether it were the refusal to go out to understand a Scotsman or the refusal to put all his humanity into the effort to understand a Jesuit, a tyrant or a poet. The fervour of the whig historian very often comes from what is really the transference into the past of an enthusiasm for something in the present, an enthusiasm for democracy or freedom of thought or the liberal tradition. But the true historical fervour is the love of the past for the sake of the past. It is the fervour that was awakened in Gibbon and Gregorovius by the sight of the ruins of ancient Rome. And behind it is the very passion to understand men in their diversity, the desire to study a bygone age in the things in which it differs from the present. The true historical fervour is that of the man for whom the exercise of historical imagination brings its own reward, in those inklings of a deeper understanding, those glimpses of a new interpretative truth, which are the historian's achievement and his æsthetic delight.

A further objection to the view of history which has been presented in this essay would be the argument that by all its implications it seems to be a kind of history that is incapable of abridgment. It might be said that there is a sense in which history cannot be truly abridged, any more than a symphony by Beethoven can, and indeed all the difficulties of the question of historical study seem to spring from this basic problem of its abridgment. If history could be told in all its complexity and detail it would provide us with something as chaotic and baffling as life itself; but because it can be condensed there is nothing that cannot be made to seem simple, and the chaos acquires form by virtue of what we choose to omit. The evils of this become apparent if we remember that much of our discussion of historical questions is concerned with a scheme of general history which we hold in our minds as our basis of reference; it is the product of a wide range of inference upon a very abridged version of the historical story. In this kind of discussion the loose thinker can achieve certainty and can reach judgments that have an air of finality, whereas a more scrupulous reflection would have much less to show for itself and might result only in tentativeness and doubt. Whatever value general history may have as a subject of popular study is greatly counterbalanced by the actual premium which it places in this way upon loose thinking. It engenders a pleasant exhilaration in the mind by reason of the facility with which it allows us to move over grand areas and exercise ourselves on momentous topics. It gives great scope to large inferences whose fallacy cannot readily be detected. It allows us to pursue in all its ramifications the wisdom that is so easy – but so dangerous – 'after the event.' It might be said that out of the dissemination of historical studies there has been born into the world a new form of nonsense, a new realm of specious generalisations and vague plausibilities, built up out of confusions of thought that were not known before, characterised by the bold handling of concepts that do not represent anything capable of genuine concrete visualisation – the whole issuing out of a process of too much argumentation upon abridged history. And it is not a mere coincidence that in history and its derivative studies this kind of cogitation has worked wonders for the whigs.

When the whig historian tells us that the Reformation led to liberty, there may be truth in his statement but this does not mean that we are justified in making any inferences from it as it stands. Such a statement may have its place as the conclusion of the historian's argument, but it is more than dangerous if we take it as the starting-point for ours. It is a great temptation to the mind to lay hold upon some such statement as this, and go sailing out to sea with it, trying to find the logical extension of which the thought is capable. We forget that the thesis as it stands represents the utmost logical extension which the historian could justifiably give to the idea he was pursuing. We fly into the sky with it when in reality it requires to be brought to earth; it ought to be subjected to an internal analysis that will disclose its underlying complexity. A great danger lies in the broad spaces over which the mind can range, playing upon the historian's half-truths; and for this reason genuine historical study is bound to be intensive, taking us away from our abridgments, not upwards to vague speculation, but downwards to concrete detail. Now if we show liberty proceeding out of Protestantism we shall have men only too ready to argue the development of modern liberty from the constitution of Protestantism itself, and their logic will be the more facile in that they will be thinking of the Protestantism of the present-day.   It is at least better to show liberty proceeding out of the clash of both Protestant and Catholic, if only for the reason that this statement of the case suggests complexity and interaction; it leaves loose threads still hanging and raises a question that can only be answered by a more intensive study.   In other words, the whig version of history particularly lends itself to generalisation and to vague philosophising; and yet by these very qualities it is a dangerous foundation upon which to build this kind of reasoning.

It is perhaps a tragedy that the important work of abridging history is so often left to writers of text-books and professional manufacturers of commercial literature.   It is unfortunate that so many abridgments of history are in reality not abridgments at all — not the condensation of a full mind but mere compilations from other abridgments.   It would seem that abridgments are often falsified by the assumption that the essentials of the story can be told, leaving out the complications;

an assumption which overlooks the fact that history is the whole network produced by countless complications perpetually involving one another. There is a danger that abridgments may be based more or less consciously upon some selective principle, as is the case with the whig interpretation which organises the whole course of centuries upon what is really a directing principle of progress. There is a danger in all abridgments that acquire certainty by reason of what they omit, and so answer all questions more clearly than historical research is ever able to do. Finally there is the undoubted danger that we may pile too heavy a weight of inference upon the general statements of historians — statements from which all that complicates and qualifies has been abbreviated out of existence. These are the abuses of abridged history, but when all has been said they are only its abuses; they show how history-books may teach the reverse of what history teaches, and they show why history can so often be turned into propaganda; but they do not alter the fact that there never was a work of history that did not greatly abridge, and indeed they support the

assertion that in the work of actual composition the art of the historian is precisely the art
of abridgment; his problem is this problem.

What we have the right to demand of him is
that he shall not change the meaning and purport of the historical story in the mere act of
abridging it, that by the selection and organising of his facts there shall not be interpolated
a theory, there shall not be interposed a new
pattern upon events, particularly one that
would never be feasible if all the story were
told in all its detail.   If the general impression
that emerges from history is the impression
of the complexity of the interactions which
produced the modern world, then the abridgment may be as simple as it likes, but it must
be an exposition in some form or another of
complexity.   Indeed the historian is never
more himself than when he is searching his
mind for a general statement that shall in itself
give the hint of its own underlying complexity.
And the problem of abridgment is the problem of abridging a complexity.   It is something more than a mechanical question of what
to put in and what to leave out; it is also
the organic question of how to reduce details

without losing the purport and tenor of the whole. All abridgment is a kind of impressionism – though the historian may be the last person to be conscious of it – and it implies the gift of seeing the significant detail and detecting the sympathies between events, the gift of apprehending the whole pattern upon which the historical process is working. It is not the selection of facts in accordance with some abstract principle; for, if it were, the abstract principle would beg all questions and we should be in a position to impose any pattern we liked upon the story. It is the selection of facts for the purpose of maintaining the impression – maintaining, in spite of omissions, the inner relations of the whole. Great work has been done in this form of abridged history when the master of some historical period has condensed into a few pages his apprehension of the workings of events, his exposition of their interplay; and has managed to communicate to the reader those weavings of the historical process which make the texture of the period. And by this we recognise the virtue of his history; that in his abridgment he has still maintained the texture.

Finally, it might be objected that nothing could be more painful than to prevent the historian from commenting upon his story as he tells it; that the historian has the right to make judgments, even though these might be only a digression; and that we have him unfairly muzzled if we do not grant him the pleasure of delivering his *obiter dicta*. He is entitled to dwell affectionately upon this personality or that episode, if only for the purpose of producing a fine period; and it is lawful for him to launch into denunciations, if only for the sake of warming the reader to his subject. His comments on life or politics or people will be valuable in proportion to his own insight, and according to their depth and acuteness we shall adjudge him a more or less profound historian. All this is true, and it is certain that the real value of a piece of historical writing will come from the richness and fullness of the mind which the historian has brought to his work; but this is to say that such comments and such judgments are those of the historian himself; their value is the measure of his acuteness; their bias is the clue to the inclinations of his mind. They are not the judgments of history, they are the opinions of the historian. In other words, they are a personal matter, and one might say that they are subject to no law. The historian may be cynical with Gibbon or sentimental with Carlyle; he may have religious ardour or he may be a humorist. He may run through the whole gamut of the emotions, and there is no reason why he should not meet history in any or all of the moods that a man may have in meeting life itself. It is not sin in a historian to introduce a personal bias that can be recognised and discounted. The sin in historical composition is the organisation of the story in such a way that bias cannot be recognised, and the reader is locked along with the writer in what is really a treacherous argument in a circle. It is to abstract events from their context and set them up in implied comparison with the present day, and then to pretend that by this 'the facts' are being allowed to 'speak for themselves.' It is to imagine that history as such, or historical research however intense, or historical surveys however broad, can give us judgments of value – to assume that this ideal or that person can be proved to have been wrong by the mere lapse of time.

It may happen that the last word of the historian, pondering upon the results of his study, may be some comment on a principle of progress that lies below everything else in the processes of time, or may be some estimate of the contribution which the whig party has made to our development, or may be an appreciation of the religious genius of Martin Luther. But this is not by any means to be confused with the whig method of selecting facts and organising the story upon a principle that begs all questions. And the conclusions will be very different from those which are arrived at when all problems are solved by the whig historian's rule of thumb. The conclusions will be richer by reason of the very distance that has had to be travelled in order to attain them.

VI. MORAL JUDGMENTS IN HISTORY

It is the natural result of the whig historian's habits of mind and his attitude to history — though it is not a necessary consequence of his actual method — that he should be interested in the promulgation of moral judgments and should count this as an important part of his office. His preoccupation is not difficult to understand when it is remembered that he regards himself as something more than the enquirer. By the very finality and absoluteness with which he has endowed the present he has heightened his own position. For him the voice of posterity is the voice of God and the historian is the voice of posterity. And it is typical of him that he tends to regard himself as the judge when by his methods and his equipment he is fitted only to be the detective. His concern with the sphere of morality forms in fact, the extreme point in his desire to make judgments of value, and to count them as the verdict of history. By a curious example of the transference of ideas he, like many other people, has come to confuse the importance which courts of legal justice must hold, and the finality they must have for practical reasons in society, with the most useless and unproductive of all forms of reflection – the dispensing of moral judgments upon people or upon actions in retrospect.

And it is interesting to see that the same mind and temper which induced the first act of self-aggrandisement, tend quickly to lead to another one, which is unobtrusive, indefinite, unavowed. The assertiveness which in the first place claimed the prerogatives of eternal justice, now proceeds by a similar logic to a more subtle form of encroachment; for the whig historians have shown a propensity to heighten the colouring of their historical narrations by laying hold on some difference of opinion or some conflict of policies and claiming this as a moral issue. And indeed it is a propensity which requires great self-discipline in any of us to resist. It must be remembered that there are some things in the past which the whig is very anxious to condemn, and some of his views have a way of turning themselves into something like a moral code. There is at least a chance that the real burden of his indignation may fall on things which are anathema only to the whigs. It is not an accident that he has shown a disinclination to see moral judgments removed from history.

It might be true to say that in Lord Acton, the whig historian reached his highest consciousness; and it is true, and at the same time it is not a mere coincidence, that in his writings moral judgments appeared in their most trenchant and uncompromising form, while in his whole estimate of the subject the moral function of history was most greatly magnified. One may gather from his statements in this connection that he regarded this side of his thought as the consequence of his Catholicism; but one may question his self-analysis at this point, for it is difficult to see that either the actual content of his moral code (as it can be inferred from what might be called his judicial decisions), or the particular way in which he applied his principles to any case that was under consideration, could be regarded as representing a system that was

specifically Catholic or Christian. It is not
malicious to suggest that they should be put
down rather to his bias as a whig historian.
When, in defence of his position, he made the
remark that 'Power tends to corrupt and
absolute power corrupts absolutely,' he may
have been stating the wisest of truths, but we
can suspect that it was a truth more dear to
the heart of the liberal that there was in him
than to the mind of the Roman Catholic; and
though the thesis is one which might serve to
excuse and explain as much as to condemn a
historical personage, it is put forward with a
hostile innuendo, it is given as the reason why
no allowance is to be made for men in high
places. Acton refers with implied approval
to a view of history which his theories really
elaborate, and he describes this view as
follows: 'It deems the canonisation of the
historic past more perilous than ignorance or
denial, because it would perpetuate the reign
of sin and acknowledge the sovereignty of
wrong.' It is curious, though it is not incom-
prehensible, that a professor should find it
necessary to warn young historians against an
excess of sympathy or appreciation for the

historic past; but what is more interesting is the thorough whig bias that is obvious though latent in the remark. Most illuminating of all would be to pursue if it were possible the connotations in the mind of the whig historian of the words, 'the reign of sin . . . the sovereignty of wrong,' particularly as they are flavoured by their reference to 'the canonisation of the past.' Finally, in this, as in many more of Acton's theses, we find some sign of what is a common feature of whig historians; there is the hint that for all this desire to pass moral judgments on various things in the past, it is really something in the present that the historian is most anxious about. Another statement of Acton's is interesting and is perhaps very acute; it is to the effect that much more evil is due to conscious sin and much less to unconscious error than most of us are usually aware; though whatever its value may be it can scarcely be regarded as a lesson of history, for it is an extreme example of the kind of truth that can only be reached by self-analysis. Coupled with another statement it becomes extremely dangerous; for Acton in his Inaugural Lecture gives reasons why it is better that the sin should be presumed than that we should search too far for other explanations. 'There is a popular saying of Madame de Staël,' he writes, 'that we forgive whatever we really understand. The paradox has been judiciously pruned by her descendant, the Duc de Broglie, in the words: "Beware of too much explaining, lest we end by too much excusing."' Once again a whig theory of history has the practical effect of curtailing the effort of historical understanding. An undefined region is left to the subjective decision of the historian, in which he shall choose not to explain, but shall merely declare that there is sin. One can only feel that if a historian holds such a combination of theories, there must have been something in the past or the present which he very badly wanted to condemn. In fact, there is too much zest in the remark: 'Suffer no man and no cause to escape the undying penalty which history has the power to inflict on wrong.' The whig historian, like Aquinas – if indeed it was Aquinas – may find perhaps too great comfort in the contemplation of some form of torment for the damned.

But it would be unjust to Lord Acton to
overlook the fact that behind his views on
moral judgments there lies a more fundamental thesis.   Acton held a very attractive
theory concerning the moral function of history.   It is perhaps the highest possible form
of the whig tendency to exalt historical study.
To Bishop Creighton Acton wrote that when
the historian makes a compromise on the
question of moral principles, history ceases to
be an 'arbiter of controversy, the upholder
of that moral standard which the powers of
earth and religion itself tend constantly to
depress.'   When history tampers with the
moral code, 'it serves where it ought to reign.'
It is an attractive exaltation of history, which
gives it the power to bind and loosen, to be the
arbiter of controversy, to reign and not to
serve; but one may believe that it is a theory
which takes too short a cut to the absolute.
It is history encroaching like the Hegelian
state, till it becomes all-comprehensive, and
stands as the finality in a moral world; taking
custody of that moral standard which 'religion
itself tends constantly to depress.'   It is history
raised into something like the mind of God,

making ultimate judgments upon the things which are happening in time. Here is the true Pope, that will not be *servus servorum Dei*; here is the only absolutism that the whig is disposed to defend; here is divine right and non-resistance, for (if a word can be allowed in malice) is not history on the side of the whigs? It is not easy to resist the temptation to personify and idealise history, and there is no doubt that this species of romancing has its effect upon the posture of the historian. In its practical consequences it means the exaltation of the opinions of the historian. It reaches its highest point in the conception of history as the arbiter, history as the seat of judgment, particularly on moral issues. Lord Acton carried it to the extremity of its logical conclusion. 'It is the office of historical science to maintain morality as the sole impartial criterion of men and things.' 'To develop and perfect and arm conscience is the great achievement of history.'

Acton, however, did not exactly set out to defend the moral function of the historian against the unbeliever. He was concerned rather with the manner in which this function

should be construed and the seriousness with
which this duty should be carried out. He
was attacking the historian who, while taking
for granted that moral judgments were part of
his province, used his prerogatives to make
easy exonerations and dealt loosely with the
moral code. Much of his doctrine is a valid
protest against the slipshod nature of the excuses that can be adduced by the historian,
particularly when these excuses are mechanic-
ally applied to any given case. And he raises
the serious question how far a historian's
explanations – such as the reference to a man's
upbringing or to 'the spirit of the age' – can
really exonerate an offender, for example, a
Pope in the fifteenth century of the Christian
era. When all historical explanations of
character and conduct have been exhausted,
it must be remembered that the real moral
question is still waiting to be solved; and what
can the historian do about the secret recesses
of the personality where a man's final moral
responsibility resides? Acton sees the problem, but he merely says that in cases of doubt
we should incline to severity. This is the
meaning of his statement that more evil is due

to conscious sin, and less is due to unconscious error than many people are aware. And this is why he can say 'Beware of too much explaining lest we end by too much excusing.' Granted that the historian has raised the moral question at all, and has accepted the assumptions which the very raising of the question must imply, he must not then slide down from this lofty moral sphere and fall back into the terms of his own historical world, thereby easing off into a different set of assumptions altogether. And in particular when he has given what is really only the historical explanation of character or conduct, he must not imagine that by this he has done anything to explain moral responsibility away. Acton puts his finger on the very centre of the problem of moral judgments in history; he is unsatisfactory because he cannot answer it; at the crucial point he can merely tell us to incline to severity. His attitude on this special question, therefore, really involves as a fundamental thesis: 'Better be unjust to dead men than give currency to loose ideas on questions of morals.' It is in fact the *reductio ad absurdum* of moral judgments in history. Acton, by focusing attention upon the real problem of these moral judgments, came very near to providing us with the argument against having them at all. Our only refuge against the impossible dilemma and the impossible ideal which his theories present to us, lies in the frank recognition of the fact that there are limits to what history and the historian can do. For the very thing with which they are concerned is the historical explanation of character and conduct, and if we distrust or discourage this kind of explanation, as even Acton seemed inclined to do, we are running perilously near to the thesis: 'Better be unhistorical than do anything that may lower the moral dignity of history.' The truth is that this historical explaining does not condemn; neither does it excuse; it does not even touch the realm in which words like these have meaning or relevance; it is compounded of observations made upon the events of the concrete world; it is neither more nor less than the process of seeing things in their context. True, it is not for the historian to exonerate; but neither is it for him to condemn. It greatly clears his mind if he can forgive all sins without denying that there are sins to forgive; but remembering that the problem of their sinfulness is not really a historical problem at all. And though it is certainly not in his competence to declare that moral responsibility does not exist, we may say that this responsibility lies altogether outside the particular world where the historian does historical thinking. He is faced with insuperable difficulties if he tries to stand with one foot in a world that is not his own.

Granting — what is less easy than might appear — an agreement on points of morality, it is a subtle matter to find the incidence of these upon any particular case. And it must be remembered that moral judgments are by their very nature absolute; in the sense that it is pointless to make them unless one can claim definitely to be right. It may be easy for the moralist of the twentieth century to discuss the ethics of persecution, to say perhaps that religious persecution would be wrong to-day, perhaps that it was wrong in all the ages. It may be easy to judge the thing, to condemn the act, but how shall the historian pass to the condemnation of people, and apply his standards to the judgment of a special incident at

any particular moment? Shall he say that in
the 16th century all men are absolved, because
the age took persecution for granted and
counted it a duty; or shall he condemn men
for not being sufficiently original in their
thoughts to rise above the rules and standards
of their own day? Shall he condemn Mary
Tudor as a persecutor and praise Catherine
de' Medici for seeking toleration, or is it more
true to say that Mary was fervent and consistent in her Catholicism, while Catherine was
more worldly and indifferent? The historian's function is in the first place to describe
the persecutions for which the English queen
was responsible, and to narrate the attempts
of the French queen to secure toleration; but
because he has the art of sifting sources and
weighing evidence, this does not mean that
he has the subtlety to decide the incidence of
moral blame or praise. He is the less a
historian certainly if by any moral judgment
he puts a stop to his imaginative endeavour,
and if through moral indignation he cuts short
the effort of historical understanding. Faced
with the poisonings of which Alexander VI
is accused, it is for the historian to be merely

interested, merely curious to know how such things came to happen. It is his duty to show why Mary persecuted and why Catherine did not wish to, until it seems natural to us that the one should have done the one thing while the other acted differently. Perhaps in proportion as he sets out to show why a certain event took place and how a certain deed came to be done, he actually disarms our moral judgment, and makes an end of the very impulse to moral indignation. By setting himself the task of explaining how Mary Tudor came to be what she was, he makes moral judgments for the time being utterly irrelevant. The truth is that the historian, whose art is a descriptive one, does not move in this world of moral ideas. His materials and his processes, and all his apparatus exist to enable him to show how a given event came to take place. Who is he to jump out of his true office and merely announce to us that it ought never to have happened at all ?

The complications to which the exercise of moral judgment may lead us are illustrated in the case of Napoleon Bonaparte. Napoleon claimed that by his genius and by his destiny he was cut off from the moral world. He considered himself an exception to the usual rules concerning right and wrong, and seems to have been conscious that he was a strange creature fallen among the habitations of men, a completely a-moral person working with the indifference of a blind force in nature – something like an avalanche that had crashed upon the world. It is true that he was not indifferent to morality in other people. It was almost his vocation to restore a moral order that had collapsed in the Revolution, to discipline society again, and to bring back the decencies of life. But this was consistent with his claim to be outside the moral order, because he considered that he himself was so to speak the moral end, as the Hegelian state claims to be. He believed that it was in serving him that other men attained their own good. All that he did in his own interests he could count as done for the glory of France. All that endangered his position was a menace to the state. His situation and his power combined with his instinct to make him avowedly the a-moral man.

When a person has so completely stated his

own outlawry from the moral order, it is
tautology for a historian to do anything but
describe his own view of himself. It is either
redundant or it is extremely subtle to discuss
the morality of a man who does not admit the
moral order, or regards himself as an exception
to its laws. And when a man has so completely stated his whole position, it is not very
useful to go on to discuss whether any particular deed of his must be considered immoral.
If he claims to be outside morality, it is much
more relevant to study his errors; for when a
man says that he himself is the state it is essen-
tial that he should not make mistakes. If the
execution of the Duc d'Enghien was necessary
for the maintenance of Napoleon's government, one might argue that it was necessary
for the stability and the peace of France; and
in this case it raises the tangled question of
what one may do to ensure the safety of the
state. But, if Napoleon were mistaken, and
if the execution was not necessary for that
purpose, then the error itself was immoral-
ity, and it is not mere callous indifference
to say that the mistake was worse than a
crime.

But moral judgments are useless unless they can be taken to imply a comparison of one man with another. Otherwise, the historian would have to fall flat with the commonplace that all men are sinners sometimes. At the same time it is impossible to make comparisons of this kind unless we compare also the situation in which men find themselves — the urgency of their position, the purposes for which they were working, the demands which they were willing to make upon themselves at the time when they made their claims on others. It is difficult again to judge a man like Napoleon, who stood so to speak in the free air and had the power to do what he liked. No government controlled his actions; no law or police kept him within the rails; no institutions set the limiting conditions for his moral behaviour; no fear of social disapproval held him back. All the forces which curb the selfishness of all of us, and the circumstances which even limit our desires, were so to speak beneath his hand, and left him free and unconditioned. It is impossible for us even to imagine a man whose situation and power leave him free to choose his conduct and let loose desire — free to do

with other men as he pleases. We do not
know that the Prussian king would have been
more moderate in his ambitions if he had had
the power to carry them out and the chance
ever to make free play with his mind. And
we do not know that we, who because of our
circumstances, have small desires and a
thousand automatic repressions of desire,
would have been more respectable than he
in our lives, if we had been in a position to
range over the whole universe of desire. We
know, indeed, that this man, whose mind was
in some ways so unbridled, did not live without performing upon himself what were
marvels of self-discipline. This is not a
defence of Napoleon, who knew that his
career was a scourge to the whole continent.
And these things do not eliminate the moral
responsibility upon which Lord Acton set
such store. But they do show that Napoleon
is not to the historian the object of a simple
and absolute moral judgment. They make it
necessary for us to translate the whole question
into terms with which the historian is competent to deal. We are in the world that is the
historian's own if we say that the character of

Napoleon is to him the subject of a piece of description.

It is not his function to tease himself with questions concerning the place where moral responsibility resides; concerning the extent to which ends justify means and good causes cover wicked actions; or concerning the degree to which a man may go in Machiavellianism to save perhaps the very existence of a state. But he can give evidence that Napoleon lied, that Alexander VI poisoned people and that Mary Tudor persecuted; and to say that one man was a coward, or another man a fanatic, or a certain person was an habitual drunkard may be as valid as any other historical generalisation. The description of a man's characteristics, the analysis of a mind and a personality are, subject to obvious limits, part of the whole realm of historical interpretation; for it is the assumption of historical study that by sympathy and insight and imagination we can go at least some way towards the understanding of people other than ourselves and times other than our own. Further, the historian may concern himself with the problem which seems to have troubled Lord Acton:

the effect which the promulgation of slipshod
ideas on moral questions may have had at any
time upon human conduct. The historian is
on his own ground again when he enquires
into the consequences at certain periods in the
past of various forms of the doctrine that the
end justifies the means; or when he shows the
historical importance of various ethical theories
that concern the state. When Acton asserts
that there has been little 'progress in ethics . . .
between St. John and the Victorian era,' he
may be right or wrong, but he is making what
we might call a historical statement. Ethical
questions concern the historian in so far as they
are part of the world which he has to describe;
ethical principles and ideals concern him only
in the effect they have had on human beings;
in other words, he deals with morality in so far
as it is a part of history. If morality is the
product of history, the historian may be called
upon to describe its development. If it is an
absolute system, equally binding on all places
at all times, then it does not concern him, for
his apparatus only allows him to examine the
changes of things which change. But even in
this case, it is only the form of the question

which is required to be re-stated; he will be driven now to watch the story of men's growing consciousness of the moral order, or their gradual discovery of it. Morality, even though it be absolute, is not absolute to him.

Taking the broad history of centuries, it is possible to watch the evolution of constitutional government and religious liberty, and one may see this evolution as the co-operative achievement of all humanity, whig and tory assisting in spite of themselves, Protestant and Catholic both necessary to the process, the principles of order and liberty making perpetual interaction, and, on both sides of the great controversies, men fighting one another who were considered good in their day, and who, to the historian, are at any rate 'irreproachable in their private lives.' But if the historian is prepared to discriminate between the purposes for which well-meaning men fought one another, and if he is prepared to see the issue as a moral issue and make it a matter for an absolute judgment, if he insists that it is his business to treat his subject in a realm of moral ideas, he will certainly find a shorter cut to whatever purpose he is working

for, and his history will be written in stronger
lines, for it will be a form of the whig over-
dramatisation.   He may then hold liberty and
constitutional government as issues in the
perennial clash of the principles of good and
evil.   He may make ancient quarrels his own
and set humanity for ever asunder, and,
judging the past by the present, keep all
generations for ever apart.   And it has happened that he has been able to admit that
there were good men on both sides of the
great conflict, but to do it without making the
least sacrifice of what must be regarded as the
luxury and pleasing sensuousness of moral
indignation.   Behind everything, and not-
withstanding something like a cosmic scheme
of good and evil in conflict, the whig historian
has found it possible to reserve for himself one
last curious piece of subtlety.   He can choose
even to forgive the private life of Fox and
save his moral condemnation for 'the repres-
sive policy of Pitt.'   For of Lord Acton himself we are informed that 'he had little desire
to pry into the private morality of kings and
politicians'; and it was Acton who told historians that they must 'suspect power more

than vice.' The whig seems to prefer to take his moral stand upon what he calls the larger questions of public policy. So upon the whig interpretation of history we have imposed the peculiar historian's ethics, by which we can overlook the fact that a king is a spendthrift and a rake, but cannot contain our moral passions if a king has too exalted a view of his own office. Burke's dictum, which Acton endorses, that 'the principles of true politics are those of morality enlarged,' may contain a world of truth, but it can be dangerous in the hands of the historian. And not the least of its dangers lies in the fact that it can be so easily inverted.

The historian presents us with the picture of the world as it is in history. He describes to us the whole process that underlies the changes of things which change. He offers this as his explanation, his peculiar contribution to our knowledge of ourselves and of human affairs. It represents his special mode of thought, which has laws of its own and is limited by his apparatus. If he postures good against evil, if he talks of 'the reign of sin, the sovereignty of wrong,' he sets all the angles of his picture differently, for he sets them by measurements which really come from another sphere. If he deals in moral judgments at all he is trying to take upon himself a new dimension, and he is leaving that realm of historical explanation, which is the only one he can call his own. So we must say of him that it is his duty to show how men came to differ, rather than to tell a story which is meant to reveal who is in the right. It must be remembered that, by merely enquiring and explaining, he is increasing human understanding, extending it to all the ages, and binding the world into one. And in this, rather than in the work of 'perfecting and arming conscience,' we must seek the achievement and the function and the defence of history.

Finally, against Acton's view that history is the arbiter of controversy, the monarch of all she surveys, it may be suggested that she is the very servant of the servants of God, the drudge of all the drudges. The historian ministers to the economist, the politician, the diplomat, the musician; he is equally at the service of the strategist and the ecclesiastic and the administrator. He must learn a great deal from all of these before he can begin even his own work of historical explanation; and he never has the right to dictate to any one of them. He is neither judge nor jury; he is in the position of a man called upon to give evidence; and even so he may abuse his office and he requires the closest cross-examination, for he is one of those 'expert witnesses' who persist in offering opinions concealed within their evidence. Perhaps all history-books hold a danger for those who do not know a great deal of history already. In any case, it is never safe to forget the truth which really underlies historical research: the truth that all history perpetually requires to be corrected by more history. When everything has been said, if we have not understanding, the history of all the ages may bring us no benefit; for it may only give us a larger canvas for our smudging, a wider world for our wilfulness. History is all things to all men. She is at the service of good causes and bad. In other words she is a harlot and a hireling, and for this reason she best serves those who suspect her most. Therefore, we must beware even of saying, 'History says . . .' or 'History proves . . .,' as though she herself were the oracle; as though indeed history, once she had spoken, had put the matter beyond the range of mere human enquiry. Rather we must say to ourselves: 'She will lie to us till the very end of the last cross-examination.' This is the goddess the whig worships when he claims to make her the arbiter of controversy. She cheats us with optical illusions, sleight-of-hand, equivocal phraseology. If we must confuse counsel by personifying history at all, it is best to treat her as an old reprobate, whose tricks and juggleries are things to be guarded against. In other words the truth of history is no simple matter, all packed and parcelled ready for handling in the market-place. And the understanding of the past is not so easy as it is sometimes made to appear.

EUROPEAN HISTORY TITLES IN
NORTON PAPERBOUND EDITIONS

Menéndez Pidal, Ramón. *The Spaniards in Their History.* N353

Newhouse, John. *Collision in Brussels: The Common Market Crisis of 30 June 1965.*

Nichols, J. Alden. *Germany After Bismarck: The Caprivi Era, 1890-1894.* N463

Pirenne, Henri. *Early Democracies in the Low Countries.* N565

Rowse, A. L. *Appeasement.* N139

Russell, Bertrand. *Freedom versus Organization: 1814-1914.* N136

Sontag, Raymond J. *Germany and England: Background of Conflict, 1848-1894.* N180

Stansky, Peter and William Abrahams. *Journey to the Frontier: Two Roads to the Spanish Civil War.* N509

Talmon, J. L. *The Origins of Totalitarian Democracy.* N510

Taylor, A. J. P. *Germany's First Bid for Colonies, 1884-1885.* N530

Thompson, J. M. *Louis Napoleon and the Second Empire.* N403

Tucker, Robert C. *The Marxian Revolutionary Idea.* N539

Waite, Robert G. L. *Vanguard of Nazism: The Free Corps Movement in Postwar Germany, 1918-1923.* N181

Wheeler-Bennett, John W. *Brest-Litovsk: The Forgotten Peace, March 1918.* N576

Whyte, A. J. *The Evolution of Modern Italy.* N298

Wolfers, Arnold. *Britain and France between Two Wars.* N343

Wolf, John B. *Louis XIV.*

Wolff, Robert Lee. *The Balkans in Our Time.* N305

Zeldin, Theodore. *The Political System of Napoleon III.* N580

THE NORTON HISTORY OF
MODERN EUROPE

Rice, Eugene F., Jr. *The Foundations of Early Modern Europe, 1460-1559*

Dunn, Richard S. *The Age of Religious Wars, 1559-1689*

Krieger, Leonard. *Kings and Philosophers, 1689-1789*

Breunig, Charles. *The Age of Revolution and Reaction, 1789-1850*

Rich, Norman. *The Age of Nationalism and Reform, 1850-1890*

Gilbert, Felix. *The End of the European Era, 1890 to the Present*